FUNDAMENTALS OF SOCIAL STATISTICS

Adam J. McKee

University of Arkansas – Monticello

DON'T PANIC.

To my lovely wife, Dyneia, who kindly tolerates me writing books that will never be profitable in economic terms.

CONTENTS

Preface

As a professor of criminal justice, it seems a bit ironic that I have taught statistics more than any other course in the curriculum. This certainly wasn't part of my life plan, but I have enjoyed it nonetheless. Over the many iterations of my course, I have substantially modified how I approach the problem of making statistics approachable. I major impediment to student success has been that at some time in the distant past, some nefarious person started the vicious rumor that statistics is a form of mathematics. It may be to some, but not in my building. We, social scientists, are (for the most part) not mathematicians, and that is not our approach to thinking about the topic. For most social scientists, statistics is merely one tool in the research toolbox that is useful in helping us answer certain questions about the world we live in, and the people we live with.

This text is designed to provide a gentle, student-friendly introduction to a much-maligned topic. Statistical literacy is important for the social scientist and the behavioral scientist because it is the way we provide answers to probing questions with a higher degree of objectivity. It is an aid to scientific rigor. Another critical reason to learn basic statistics is that in today's world, "big data" and "predictive analytics" are becoming a bigger part of our everyday lives. The Cambridge Analytics scandal was politically important and financially important to Facebook, but it has much broader implications. The use of information (data) indiscriminately by rogue corporations, governments, and individuals has the potential to cause untold social harm. If you have a grasp of the basic concepts of predictive modeling, you will understand some of the issues far better than most.

This text is designed to complement my growing Open Educational Resource (OER) collection. My eventual plan is to have all of my resources available for free as HTML files on my website and offer Kindle versions and print versions at the lowest possible prices. I have used this model successfully in the past, and I believe it is a good one.

A Note to the Professors

As a "one-man show," the development of my OER resources is sporadic and I freely admit that my materials lack the polish of professionally edited work. Rather than strive for perfection and thus never accomplish anything, I have decided that my personal benchmark will be *usefulness*. Since we all view our content differently, I may well have omitted something that you feel is vital, and I may have oversimplified something to the point that you think the presentation misrepresents the topic. As OER material, every version (other than the obvious print exception) can be updated in short order.

I often get emails from colleagues concerning ancillary materials. My ultimate goal is to have test banks available, as well as PowerPoint slides for each topic. If you have any comments, criticisms, or suggestions about the text or any of the ancillary materials, please send them to me at mckee@uamont.edu. And if you do find this material useful, please send me a note explaining how you are using it. If you find it unacceptable, please send me a note explaining that as well. When you work essentially for free, you want to feel that it is accomplishing some good in the world. I am always willing to make beneficial changes toward my ultimate goal of student success. As we all know, publication is a critical aspect of university life, and I will try to make the argument that adoption of my materials by colleagues suggests that they are making a bona fide contribution to the field. If I cannot accomplish this, I fear that I one day will not have the time to work on these worthwhile projects.

Adam J. McKee

Chapter 1:
Basic Concepts

Section 1.1: Statistics and the Social Sciences

For many students, *statistics* is a dirty word, second only in evil to *college algebra*. It is something mathematical developed by sadistic college professors to make undergraduate students suffer, and has no application in the real world. Its purpose is to make life hard. This could not be further from the truth! The actual purpose of statistics is to make life easy by simplifying and organizing information.

Most of us think of statistics as facts and figures—things like RBIs in baseball, the average temperature in July, and the number of deaths caused by drunk driving last year. Statistics is that and much more. We will define **statistics** as a set of rules and techniques for organizing, summarizing, and interpreting empirical information.

> **Statistics** is a set of rules and techniques for organizing, summarizing, and interpreting empirical information.

Statistics also allows us to test our ideas about how the social world works. In fact, social scientists could not search for answers to many of our most compelling questions without statistical tools. To better understand this statement, it will be helpful to recall how social scientists answer questions about the social world.

The Nature of Social Science

One of the most important things to remember about science is that the scientific method is *empirical*. **Empirical** means based on observation. In addition to observing, scientists make *systematic* observations. By **systematic,** I mean that the scientist observes with a plan, and the plan is designed to ensure objectivity. **Objectivity** means that the scientist takes steps to record facts that are not colored by emotion and personal prejudice. Recording observations as numerical measurements greatly aid the researcher in maintaining objectivity.

Empirical means based on observation rather than other methods of knowing, such as reliance on authority or "common sense."

This method presents a problem. All of these observations result in huge amounts of numbers. We can organize those numbers into a table form such as a spreadsheet, but there will still be pages and pages of them. Information (**data**) presented in this way is meaningless! The human mind simply cannot wrap itself around large amounts of numbers like that and draw anything meaningful from them. We need to organize and simplify the data. Organizing, simplifying, and summarizing data is a primary function of **descriptive statistics**.

Descriptive statistics are a family of statistical methods that organize, simplify, and summarize data.

Within the scope of empirical research, there are several strategies that the social scientist can use to answer questions. An important distinction is between whether the research is *descriptive, relational,* or *experimental*.

Descriptive research seeks to describe the characteristics of a particular social phenomenon. Researchers doing descriptive research ask, "What is the state of things?" Public opinion polls are an example of descriptive research. They answer questions about how people feel about particular issues. To be merely descriptive, the researcher treats these opinions independently and does not consider how these relate to other variables and does not offer up any potential causes.

Relational research seeks to understand how two or more variables are related. If our pollster in the above example examined how religious preference was related to whether a voter was going to vote Democrat or Republican, the study would be relational. This is because the researcher is examining the relationship between religious preference and voting preference.

Experimental research seeks to make causal statements about how the social world works. That is, the researcher wants to make cause and effect statements. Did a university's alcohol awareness program (cause) reduce incidents of alcohol-related crime on campus (effect)? Note that the confidence with which a researcher can make such statements relies heavily on good experimental design, which is beyond the scope of this text. We will focus strictly on the statistical concerns of good research design.

Note that these types of research are not mutually exclusive. In the practical world of research, they tend to work in concert, building on each other. A researcher conducting an experiment to demonstrate that one variable causes another will no doubt want to describe both variables and explain how they are related as well. In other words, these divisions are somewhat arbitrary, but they are useful because each has a set of statistical techniques that goes along with it. Descriptive statistics are heavily used in descriptive research, and inferential statistics are used heavily in experimental research. Relational research uses a family of *correlational* statistics that can be both descriptive and inferential depending on how they are treated.

Descriptive statics, then, seek to summarize and explain the characteristics of a variable. The other major branch of statistics, *inferential statistics*, lets the researcher make generalizations about a *population* given information from a *sample*. **Generalizations** are general statements obtained by *inference* from specific cases.

> **Generalizations** are general concepts that come from inferences from specific cases.

An **inference** is a conclusion that is based on facts and reasoning. We can gather from these definitions that the purpose of **inferential statistics** is to let us make general statements about populations based on information that we have gathered from samples.

> **Inferential statistics** is the branch of statistics that uses sample data to reach conclusions (make inferences about) populations.

To understand the jargon of inferential statistics, it is helpful to understand how social scientists answer most questions. It is important to understand that scientists are generally interested in populations. A **population** is the entire group of people that a researcher is interested in making statements about. A population can be very small, such as female Supreme Court justices, or it can be very large, such as every registered voter in the United States.

> A **population** is the entire group of interest in a research study.
> A number that describes the characteristics of a population is called a **parameter**.

When a researcher collects information about an entire population, it is called a **census**. Numbers that describe characteristics of populations are known as **parameters**. For example, when the Bureau of the Census reports the median household income of Americans, that is a parameter because it is a number that came from data collected on the entire population.

*A **census** is information collected from the entire population of interest.*

When populations are large, it becomes unfeasible to collect data for every person. There simply are not enough resources (human resources, time, money, etc.) to conduct a census. When this is the case, researchers use samples. A **sample** is a subset of a population that is used to answer questions about the population from which it was drawn. Numbers that describe characteristics of samples are called **statistics**.

*A **sample** is a subset of a population that is used to answer questions about the population.*

*A number that describes the characteristics of a sample is called a **statistic.***

Social scientists using inferential statistics start with a hypothesis and look to see if data gathered from systematic observations are consistent with the *hypothesis*. Many of these techniques are complex and are best left to computers. For now, we will define a **hypothesis** as an educated guess as to how some social phenomenon occurs. (We will delve more deeply into hypotheses when we get to the sections on inferential statistics).

*A **hypothesis** is an educated guess as to how some social phenomenon occurs.*

Even if you do not plan to conduct research, you must be an intelligent consumer of research to assume a leadership role in today's data-rich world. The social science professions, even the applied ones such as social work and criminal justice, depend on social scientific research to determine best practices, prepare grant applications, conduct program evaluations, and many other management tasks. In every arena of public management, there is a growing demand for *accountability*. Accountability in a narrow but important sense means that tax dollars are spent on programs that work and work well. The public demands objective evaluations of programs and policies. Such evaluations are performed using the same techniques that social scientists use to answer other questions.

Never forget, then, that the ultimate goal of statistics is to explain real world events. This is a two part process that calls for the objective application of the statistical methods that we'll learn in this little book, and it requires subjective judgments as to what is good, what is right, and what is meaningful. Ultimately, science in general and statistical methods in general are only useful in informing the subjective judgments of decision makers. Science is not a tool for making ethical decisions, but it is a tool for informing ethical decisions makers. Statistics is a scientific tool, but the interpretation and application of that objective information is often more of an art than a science. That is why a major focus of this book is understanding *why* we compute a particular statistic, and what exactly the results mean.

Key Terms

Statistics, Descriptive Statistic, Average, Empirical, Objectivity, Data, Systematic Observation, Inferential Statistic, Sample, Population, Percentage, Margin of Error, Census, Parameter, Generalization

Section 1.2:
Basic Math Review

I n the modern world, your ability to compute the value of a t-test or and F-test is questionable. Not only can you do that with statistical software, but you can also do it with scientific calculators and spreadsheet software like Microsoft's Excel. Still, you need to know some basic math skills to understand what the results mean. In other words, you need basic math skills to interpret the computer output. Also, you will need some basic math skills to perform simple operations that translate the computer output into something that is more presentable in reports and presentations.

Addition & Subtraction

Recall from the *very* early years of your education that addition means adding a group of numbers together. Addition is almost always signified by the + symbol.

Example: $5 + 4 = 9$

Subtraction means taking the value of one number away from the value of another number. Subtraction is almost always signified by the − symbol.

Example: $8 - 4 = 4$

Note that the result of an addition problem is known as the *sum*, and the result of a subtraction problem is known as the *difference*.

Multiplication and Division

Multiplication has several symbols. The most common is probably the **x** symbol, at least in elementary schools where you learned to multiply in the first place. Others include the · and the * symbols.

When an expression is next to another and both are enclosed in parentheses, treat it as a multiplication problem.

Example: (3)(6) = 18

A division problem is also a fraction. This is the reason that the slash mark is used as the division symbol on the computer keyboard. To solve the problem, simply divide the top number by the bottom number. This is also how you convert a fraction to a proportion in order to enter it into a calculator.

Example: 18 / 3 = 6

Dealing with Negative Numbers

Most of the time in everyday life we deal with positive numbers, so your skills in dealing with negative numbers are probably rusty. Statistics is an area where we use many negative numbers, so you need to brush up on the rules. Recall something you learned a long time ago: the number line.

$$-6 \quad -5 \quad -4 \quad -3 \quad -2 \quad -1 \quad 0 \quad +1 \quad +2 \quad +3 \quad +4 \quad +5 \quad +6$$

On the number line, negative numbers run to the left of zero, and positive numbers run to the right of zero. The bigger a negative number, the further you are getting from zero and the "deeper in the hole" you get.

When a number is shown without a sign, it is assumed positive. The negative sign will precede negative numbers.

Apply the following rules when working with negative numbers:

One: When you multiply or divide numbers with different signs, the result is negative.

Two: When you multiply or divide numbers with the same signs, the results are always positive. This also means that when you square a negative number, the result will always be positive.

Three: when you add up a series of negative numbers, the result is negative.

Four: When you add a positive number and a negative number, ignore the sign and treat it as a subtraction problem, subtracting the smaller from the larger. The result takes on the sign of the larger number.

Five: If you have a series of numbers with mixed signs that need to be added together, sum all of the positive numbers, then sum all of the negative numbers, then use rule *four* above to determine the final sum.

Six: When you subtract a negative from a negative, ignore the sign and subtract. The result is negative.

Example: -10 - -4 = -6

Seven: When you subtract a negative number from a positive number, the negative number becomes a positive number and the numbers are added together.

Example: 5 - -5 = 10

Eight: When you subtract a positive number from a negative number, ignore the signs and add the numbers together. The answer is always negative.

Example: -6 – 4 = -10

Fractions, Decimals, and Percents

Remember that when you are dealing with decimals, the first place to the right of the decimal is the *tenths* place, the second place is the *hundredths* place, and the third place is the *thousandths* place, and so on. Most statistics are reported to at least the hundredths place. If there is no whole number before the decimal, it is customary to report a zero before the decimal. This calls attention to the fact that you are dealing with a number smaller than one.

Many formulas in statistics contain fractions. To understand what these formulas are doing, it is very helpful to recall the basics of fractions. Fractions can be expressed two primary ways: With a horizontal line dividing the **numerator** (the top of a fraction) and **denominator** (the bottom of a fraction), or a slash dividing the numerator and denominator.

We can also divide the numerator by the denominator and get a **proportion**, which is a fraction expressed in decimal form. We can easily convert that proportion to a **percentage** by multiplying it by 100 (which moves the decimal two places to the right).

Examples:

$$2/3 = \frac{1}{6} = 0.6667 = 66.67\%$$

$$1/2 = \frac{1}{2} = 0.5000 = 50.00\%$$

Remember the following characteristics of fractions:

- As the numerator increases, the value of the faction increases.
- As the denominator increases, the value of the fraction decreases.
- With complex fractions, perform all math operations in both the numerator and the denominator before dividing.

A **percentage** is a special fraction where the denominator is always 100, regardless of how many subjects we are describing. If we say 50% of our subjects have a particular characteristic, we are saying that 50 out of 100 have it. It may be helpful to recall that *cent* comes from Latin and means 100. By using a common denominator, percentages are very useful in allowing us to compare groups of different sizes. It also aids us in understanding the characteristics of large groups that we can't intuitively grasp.

To convert a fraction to a percent, divide the numerator by the denominator and multiply by 100.

Roots and Exponents

In statistics, there is a lot of squaring. To square a number, simply multiply the number by itself.

Example: $3^2 = 3 \times 3 = 9$

Note that we know to multiply 3 by itself in the above example because the raised up number 2—the exponent—tells us to multiply the number preceding the exponent by itself that number of times. This can also be expressed as "three to the second power."

We can raise a number to the third power, called cubing.

Example: $2^3 = 2 \times 2 \times 2 = 8$

Special Exponent Rules

-Any number raised to the first power equals itself.

-If any exponent appears outside of parentheses, then any operations inside the parentheses are done first.

-If a negative number is raised to an exponent, the result will be positive for exponents that are even and negative for exponents that are odd.

-An exponent applies only to the base that is just in front of it.

A number printed above the line like an exponent is called a **superscript**. This is the term to look for when formatting an exponent on your computer.

Taking a square root is the opposite of squaring. This means, for example, that the square root of 9 is 3. The formal name for the square root sign ($\sqrt{\ }$) is the *radical sign*.

When a radical sign appears in an equation (as it often does in statistics), it has the same effect as parentheses on the order of operations.

Example:

$$2\sqrt{20+5} = 2\sqrt{25} = 2(5) = 10$$

Order of Operations

To get the correct solution to any math problem, you must do things in the proper order. That order is dictated by the *order of operations rules*. The basic rules are as follows:

Rule one: If there are parentheses, do the stuff in parentheses first. If there are parentheses within parentheses (nested), work from the inside out.

Rule two: If there are exponents and roots, resolve them left to right.

Rule three: Do all multiplication and division, working left to right.

Rule four: do all addition and subtraction problems, working left to right.

Summation

The Greek letter sigma (Σ) is a math operator that says, "add up the" whatever comes after it. For example, if you see ΣX, it tells you to add up all the values of X. Remember that X is usually a column heading in statistics, not a single value, as is usually the case in algebra! Only the number immediately after the sigma is summed. If you are to sum the entire expression, then parentheses will be used. Other things can be summed as well using the Σ symbol. In cases where there are ordered pairs of variables labeled X and Y, you will frequently need to compute both the ΣX and ΣY. ΣX means the sum of the X scores, and ΣY means the sum of the Y scores.

Equations

An equation is a math statement that indicates that two things are identical. That is, they have the exact same value. We are all familiar with the general form of an equation:

Examples: $12 = 4 + 8$ and $1 + 1 = 2$

Note that an equation will always have an equal sign. The equal sign is like the center point of a balance. The equation will remain "true" so long as you do the same thing to both sides. If I subtract 1 from the left side of the equation, I must also subtract one from the right side in order for it to stay balanced. We can use this idea of doing the same thing to both sides of the equation to solve for an unknown quantity.

Finding the value of an unknown quantity is often called *solving the equation*. Anytime we are solving for X (as a single quantity!) we must remember that our goal is to have the unknown quantity by itself on one side of the equal sign. We accomplish this by removing all the other numbers that are on the same side as X. What this means is that we are searching for a math operation that "gets rid of" all the terms that are not the variable we are interested in solving for.

Statistical Symbols and Jargon

As with any area of study, statistics has developed its own vocabulary and sets of symbols that you must know in order to understand what you see in books and journal articles. Because statistics makes use of so many letters as symbols, some statistical material can seem incredibly complicated at first glance. Let us say, for example, that your professor has given you four quizzes, and you made the following grades: 100, 90, 80, and 90. He then asks you to figure out your average. No problem, right? All you have to do is add up the scores and divide that by how many quizzes there were (4 in this example). Now let us say our hypothetical professor is having a bad day and asks you to compute something called the *arithmetic mean*. However, to make it easier, he is going to provide you with a formula:

$$\overline{X} = \frac{\sum X}{n}$$

If you are not familiar with statistical symbols, then that equation can look intimidating, and you still do not know what an arithmetic mean is! If we break it down into everyday language, it becomes easy, because it is just the average that you already knew how to get. The arithmetic mean is what most people would refer to as the "average."

The letter X with the bar on top (pronounced "X bar" or "bar X") is the symbol for the mean of X. In statistics, X usually stands in for a group of scores rather than a particular value as it usually does in algebra. Therefore, "bar X" stands for the mean of a group (a column) of scores labeled *X*. The Greek letter sigma is known as the summation symbol that we considered in the math review. When it appears next to X as it does in the formula above, it tells us to add up all the numbers in the *X* column. The letter *n* stands for the number of elements being considered (the number of quizzes in our example). As we introduce new procedures, we will introduce new jargon and symbols that simply must be memorized. *Without knowledge of these terms and symbols, you will not be successful in your statistics course.*

Section 1.3:
Using Spreadsheets

Spreadsheets are computer programs that store and allow the user to manipulate data. The word data refers to a collection of *quantitative* (numerical) or *qualitative* (non-numerical) values. What makes spreadsheets different from other types of data storage programs is that they are in tabular form. That is, they organize the data into **rows** (going across) and **columns** (going up and down).

Spreadsheets can store many different types of data, but, in statistics, we are mostly interested in the ability to store and manipulate numeric (quantitative) data. One of the most useful features of spreadsheets is that they allow the user to perform calculations rapidly. They also allow the user to perform very complex calculations involving multiple steps. What this means for the statistics student and researcher is that spreadsheets make complicated statistical calculations as simple as specifying what columns and rows will be involved in the calculations.

Microsoft's Excel spreadsheet program is probably the best known and best-documented software of its type in the world. It is because of this near-universal availability that this text provides instructions for computing basic statistics with this particular software. Other spreadsheets (such as Google Sheets) are available, but the process will be very similar. There are also several prominent statistical packages that are designed exclusively for the statistical analysis of data. These specialized programs really shine when a researcher is using complex multivariate methods coupled with very large datasets. For learning basic statistics, the more common spreadsheet programs will work just fine.

Using Excel

Many of the statistical methods discussed in this book can be computed using Microsoft's powerful and popular spreadsheet program *Excel*. The Data Analysis ToolPak is not installed with the standard Excel setup. Look in the Tools menu. If you do not have a Data Analysis item, you will need to install the Data Analysis tools. Search Help for "Data Analysis Tools" for instructions, or see the box below for a brief explanation.

*The word **data** is actually the plural of **datum**; datum refers to a single value, while data refers to a collection of values.*

To make statistical computations in Excel, you must first learn how to use functions. A function is a formula that is predefined within Excel to accomplish a specific task. Remember that in a table of numbers such as a spreadsheet, the lines of numbers going up and down are called **columns**, and the lines of numbers going side to side are called **rows**. Let us say we want to do something simple like compute the average for a quiz taken by our statistics class. We can set up an Excel sheet to do the job as follows:

Figure 1. The Average in Excel.

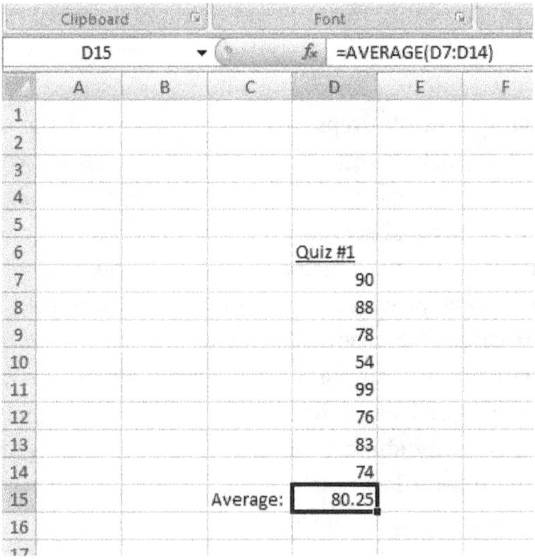

Note that all of the quiz scores are placed in a column. The value 80.25 is the average (mean). The value was not typed in, however. Excel put it there. What was typed in was the function. Functions may look a little complicated at first, but they are very easy to use once you understand the anatomy. In the function bar at the top of the table we see the syntax =**AVERAGE(D7:D14)**. *All functions in Excel begin with an equal sign.* That is how Excel knows it is a function and not just text or numbers. We could have placed the function in any cell, but it makes sense to put it at the end of the column. AVERAGE is the name of the predefined function that we are using to compute the mean. The (D7:D14) tells Excel to compute the average of the range of cells D7 through D14.

To insert a function automatically, first click on the cell where you want to place the function. Then, under the formulas tab, click insert function. This will open the insert function dialog box. Most of the functions we will be using will be found under the "statistical" category.

Visualizing Data

It is often said that "a picture paints a thousand words." There is a lot of truth to that sentiment. Often, a set of numbers makes little sense in a table, but they can come alive with meaning when presented in graphical form. **Graphs** are a visual depictions of a data set, making it easy to see patterns and other details. Deciding which type of graph to use depends on the type of data you are analyzing. Excel generally does an excellent job of producing graphs, and the controls become rather intuitive once you have mastered one type of graph. We will discuss some major types of graphs and how to generate them as we move along, but perhaps it will be helpful to get an idea of the basic types before we do move on.

Histograms: A histogram shows the distribution of data among different intervals or categories, using a series of vertical bars. For this reason, histograms are more commonly referred to as **bar charts**.

Line graphs: A line graph shows how a variable changes over time or in relation to another variable. Line graphs are made by creating a "dot plot" and then connecting the dots.

Pie charts: A pie chart shows how data are distributed between different *categories*, illustrated as a series of slices taken from a pie.

Scatter plots (scatter diagrams): A scatter plot shows the relationship between two variables as a series of points ("dots"). The pattern of the points indicates how closely related the two variables are.

Key Terms

Row, Column, Spreadsheet, Excel, Function, Data Analysis ToolPak

Important Symbols

$\Sigma Y, \Sigma X, X, \overline{X}, n$

Section 1.4:
Variables

cience attempts to discover patterns in a reality that often seems chaotic. Even from the most ancient times, people have attempted to describe patterns in the world around them. Ancient peoples noted the changes of the season, changes in the phase of the moon, changes in the tide. They also noted that these things (and many others) changed in a regular pattern. In the sciences, things that change and have different values from time to time or from person to person are called **variables.**

> A **variable** is a characteristic, attribute, or condition that has different values for different individuals.

Variables may be attributes that are different for different people, such as weight, gender, religious affiliation, political affiliation, and so forth. Variables can also be conditions in the environment that can affect the results of a study, such as the time of day when an experiment takes place.

When variables are measured, researchers often identify the variables by a letter, such as X. If two variables are used, then the researcher may denote the first variable as X and the second as Y. This shorthand is useful in describing the relationships between variables. A variable is sometimes referred to as a *column of data* because of the convention of placing information for each person in rows, which makes each column form a single variable. All the variables taken together form the **data** that we analyze in a research project.

A value that does not change from person to person is called a ***constant***. The idea of constancy is closely related to the scientific concept of ***control***, which we will discuss in more detail in a later section.

*A **constant** is an attribute of a person or a condition that does not change from person to person but stays the same for every individual.*

An **attribute** is a specific value of a variable. For example, the variable gender has two attributes: male and female. Attributes are commonly referred to as a **level** of the variable. It is important to note the difference between the variable and its value for a particular individual. For example, the variable *gender* can take on two different levels: *Male* and *female*.

Independent and Dependent Variables

Special names are used for the two variables that are being studied by a researcher in an experiment. The variable that is manipulated by the researcher—the one thought to cause a change in the other—is called the **independent variable**. The variable that is observed to see if it was changed by the independent variable is called the **dependent variable**. It is called dependent because its value *depends* on the independent variable.

In an experiment, the independent variable often reflects that the researcher administered some type of *treatment*—something we do to the participants. In its simplest form, an experiment involves two groups. The first is the group that got the treatment—the **experimental group**. A second group does not get the treatment. Individuals in this group are said to be in the **control group**.

Discrete and Continuous Variables

The variables in a study can also be described in terms of the types of values that can be assigned to them. A **discrete variable** consists of separate categories that cannot be divided. Take the variable *gender* for example. Generally, you are either male or female—the categories are indivisible. Discrete variables usually define categories or are restricted to whole, countable numbers. The variable *felony convictions* is an example. Either you have been convicted of no felonies, or you have been convicted of a whole number of felonies. You cannot have been convicted of 2.78 felonies. Another common way to look at discrete variables is as counts of things.

A **continuous variable**, on the other hand, can be subdivided into an infinite (or practically infinite) number of fractional parts. *Annual household income* (measured in dollars and cents) is a good example of a continuous variable. Variables that are continuous can be imagined to be along a line (like the number line) with no obvious points of separation. Note that it will be rare for any two subjects to have the same exact score on a continuous variable.

Key Terms

Variable, Constant, Continuous, Discrete, Experimental Group, Control Group, Independent Variable, Dependent Variable, Environmental Variable, Data, Attribute (of a Variable), Level (of a Variable)

Adam J. McKee

Section 1.5:
Scales of Measurement

Variables can also be described in terms of how much information they contain. There are four **scales or levels of measurement** that do this. The levels of measurement are important in social research because they have an impact on the types of statistics we can use to simplify and describe our data. As a rule, *always use the most informative level of measurement possible.*

The **Scales of Measurement** *are a method of classifying variables according to how much information the numerical values for the variable contain.*

Nominal Scale

The **nominal scale** consists of a set of categories that provide different names for different categories. The nominal scale does not make any quantitative distinction between categories. Favorite color is an example of a variable measured on the nominal scale. We can name colors, but we cannot make any meaningful quantitative (numerical) distinction between the categories. Does blue and any greater or lesser value than red as a favorite color? No. For this reason, *favorite color* is a nominal variable.

It can be confusing when numbers represent nominal level variables. Sometimes, numbers make convenient names. Think of the numbers on athletic jerseys. So long as these numbers serve only to name a particular player and do not provide any quantitative information (such as better players getting higher numbers), then the scale is still nominal. Do not let the presence of numbers confuse you.

*The **Nominal Scale** provides only a name, and the data are neither ordered nor measured.*

Ordinal Scale

With the **ordinal scale**, not only are measurements placed in categories (as with the nominal scale), but they are also ranked in order of magnitude. Variable that are rank orders of scores are on the ordinal scale. If someone tells you, "I graduated third in my class," they are providing an example of an ordinal scale. We do not know the person's precise GPA, but we know he did better than the person graduating fourth in the class and not as good as the person graduating second. Thus, with the ordinal scale, we can put people in *order*, but we do not know the magnitude of the difference between people.

*The **Ordinal Scale** provides both a name and order information but does not provide a measure of the difference between levels, such as with ranks.*

Interval Scale

An **interval scale** of measurement consists of an ordered set of categories (as with the ordinal scale). Also, the interval scale specifies that all the intervals are the same size. That is, the spaces between points along the scale are always the same size. Take distance measured in inches for example. The distance between the 2-inch mark and the 3-inch mark on a yardstick is the exact same as the distance between the 35-inch mark and the 36-inch mark. An inch is always an inch, no matter where we find it on the scale.

*The **Interval Scale** both orders and measures data, but does not have an absolute zero.*

It is important to note that the line between the ordinal scale and the interval scale can become fuzzy when dealing with **Likert Scales**. For example, mean scores are often reported about levels of agreement with statements on a scale of 1 to 5.

Ratio Scale

The **ratio scale** provides all the information that the interval scale does. In addition, the ratio scale provides an **absolute zero** point. That is, when you reach zero, you do not have any of the variable left.

Absolute Zero *means that a score of zero indicates a complete absence of the characteristic being studied.*

Annual household income (measured in dollars) is a good example of a common ratio level variable. When you earned zero dollars last year, then you have no income.

Contrast this with temperature measured on a Fahrenheit thermometer. A measurement of zero does not mean that you have no heat left. You can keep going below zero. A Kelvin thermometer has its zero point at absolute zero. Nothing can be colder than zero degrees Kelvin. Thus, temperature, when measured on a Fahrenheit thermometer is on an interval scale. Temperature when measured on a Kelvin thermometer is on a ratio scale.

*The **Ratio Scale** orders and measures data, as well as having an absolute zero.*

Note that there is very little difference between the interval scale and the ratio scale. Most statistics that are appropriate for one are appropriate for the other. This is why you will often see both categories with a slash between them in the methodology literature.

Latent v. Observable Variables

There is a big difference between variables that we can directly observe and the more abstract variables that cannot be observed that we refer to as **constructs**. One way to look at constructs is as *nonobservables*. This is related to what are called *latent variables*. **Latent variables** are unobserved "things" that a researcher presumes to underlie an observable variable. *Intelligence* is a common example of a latent variable. We cannot directly measure intelligence, but we can observe things that we think are related to it, such as verbal ability and mathematical ability (operationalized as scores on a standardized test).

Latent variables are unobserved "things" that a researcher presumes to underlie an observable variable.

Most of the problems that social scientists are interested in are latent variables. We as social scientists are not interested in specific children hitting each other on the playground; our real concern is understanding the latent variable *aggression*. We are not interested in a child's ability to select correct responses on a test; we are interested in the latent variable *intelligence*. Generally, we cannot measure these variables. Thus, we are forced to measure behaviors that we think indicate the presence of the latent (unobservable) variable that we are interested in.

Key Terms

Scales (Levels) of Measurement, Nominal, Ordinal, Interval, Ratio, Absolute Zero, Latent Variables

Chapter 2: Collecting and Organizing Data

Section 2.1:
Probability and Samples

ocial scientists often want to answer questions about large groups of people. Gathering information about such large groups can be impossible. When this is the case, researchers often resort to using a subset of the population to answer questions about the entire population. Using samples is common in all the sciences, not just the social ones. If you need your blood sugar checked, your doctor does not remove all of your blood! She uses a sample. For this to work, the blood in the sample must be nearly identical to all of the blood in your body. When a sample reflects the characteristics of the larger group from which it was drawn, it is said to be representative. In all the sciences, a sample must be representative if it is to be used to make inferences about the larger group. This is no less true for the social sciences. When evaluating a sampling method for a research project, the most important consideration for the accuracy of the study is the representativeness of the sample.

Populations and Samples

Social science research usually begins with a question about a specific group of people. In the language of research, the entire group of people that a researcher is interested in is called a *population*.

> A **population** is the group of all the people of interest in a particular research study.

Many times, populations are large. A political scientist, for example, may be interested in every registered female voter in the United States. Sometimes, however, populations can be very small, such as when a study concerns a very small group, such as female Supreme Court justices.

A population does not always have to consist of individual people. It can be groups of people, such as a population of police departments. A population can also consist of animals, or non-living things, such as the production of a factory. A population can be anything an investigator wants to study.

Research questions are concerned with the whole population, but it is seldom feasible to collect data from an entire population. For this reason, researchers usually select a small group from among the population and limit their study to those individuals in the smaller group. This set of individuals selected from the population is called a *sample*. A sample is intended to be *representative* of the population from which it was drawn. That is, the sample should be just like the population in every way that is important to the study.

> A **sample** is a group of individuals selected from a population that serves to represent the population in a research study.

If your physician thinks you may be anemic, she may draw a sample of your blood to test your iron level. You would be upset if the doctor wanted to take out *all* of your blood to be tested! A sample is just fine so long as the blood taken out of your body is just like the blood remaining in your body. If this is the case, then we can say that the sample of blood is representative of all your blood—the *population* of blood. With blood, representativeness can be taken for granted. When it comes to selecting a group of people to represent a larger group, we have to take great care to make sure that the sample of people is a *representative sample*.

Probability

Probability theory provides a numerical framework for measuring *uncertainty*. This area is important for researchers since all inferential statistical results are ultimately based on probability theory. Understanding probability theory provides fundamental insights into all statistical methods beyond univariate descriptive statistics. Probability is heavily based on the mathematical notion of **sets**. A set is just a collection of things. These objects may be people, places, things, or numbers. Several mathematical operations may be applied to sets, such as unions, intersections, and complements. We will not delve too deeply into the mathematics of sets and probability. We must, however, understand the basic ideas of probability theory so we can understand hypothesis tests in later sections.

The **union** of two sets is a new set that contains all the elements in the original two sets. The **intersection** of two sets is a set that contains only the elements contained in both of the two original sets (if there are any.) The **complement** of a set is a set containing elements that are *not* in the original set. For example, the complement of the set of black cards in a normal deck of playing cards (cards and dice figure prominently in discussions of probability since both relate to games of *chance*) is the set containing all red cards.

Probability theory is based on a model of how random outcomes are generated, known as a **random experiment**. Note that behavioral scientists and probability mathematicians use the term "experiment" differently; in math, it just means a trial, such as one toss of the coin or one role of the dice. In social research, an experiment is a research method designed to maximize the likelihood of causal statements being correct. In probability mathematics, the outcomes are generated in such a way that all *possible* outcomes are known in advance, but the *actual* outcome is not known in advance.

We will limit our discussion of probability math to three simple rules that will help you understand the material that is to come in later sections. We will consider:

-The Addition Rule
-The Multiplication Rule
-The Compliment Rule

You use the addition rule to determine the probability of a union of two sets. The multiplication rule is used to determine the probability of an intersection of two sets. The complement rule is used to identify the probability that the outcome of a random experiment will not be an element in a specified set.

A **random variable** assigns numerical values to the outcomes of a random experiment. When you flip a coin twice, for example, you are performing a random experiment: all possible outcomes are known in advance, and the actual outcome is not known in advance. Since the coin is flipped twice, the experiment consists of two **trials**. Of course, we know that for each trial the outcome must either be a "head" or a "tail."

Probability Distributions

We will consider how to use probability distributions in some detail in later sections, but for now, we want to get an idea of what the term means. A probability distribution is a formula or a table used to assign probabilities to each possible value of a random variable X. As with variables, a probability distributions can be *discrete*, which means that X can assume one of a finite (countable) number of values, or *continuous*, in which case X can assume one of an infinite number of different values. For the coin-flipping experiment in above example, the probability distribution of X could be a simple table that shows the probability of each possible value of X, written as P(X). The symbol P(X) is read "the probability of X" and is a short hand way of saying it, especially in probability problems.

Assume that a random variable X is defined as the number of "heads" that turn up during the course of this experiment. Coin flipping examples are used so often in probability that everyone familiar with the discipline knows that **H** stands for "heads," and **T** stands for "tails." X assigns values to the outcomes of this experiment as follows:

Outcome X	
{TT}	0
{HT, TH}	1
{HH}	2

Note that the "curly brackets" are used in set notation. Each T in brackets indicates the results of a single flip, so the first result {TT} tells us that it is possible to get a result of "tails" for each of the two flips. In that case, there would be zero heads. Since one flip could come out one way and the second flip could come out the other, the {HT, TH} notation shows this, and the fact that either way it goes, there will be a result of 1 "head." Finally, both tosses could result in heads, in which case there would be two "head" results, as depicted by the notation {HH}. Since there are four equally likely possible outcomes, the probability of each would be the same as the frequency, which would be only one out of the four possible results: ¼, or .25 (25%).

X	P(X)
0	0.25
1	0.50
2	0.25

The above table represents a probability distribution for two coin flips. As we would expect, the most common result would be to have a result of one head and one tail. This is because it can happen in *two* different ways out of the possible four (2/4 = .5). Since we've defined X as the number of "heads" we have, the most probable outcome of a random experiment is X = 1.

In probability problems, the author will often specify a "fair coin" meaning that the result of "head" and "tail" are equally likely; apparently, statistics professors generally are in possession of weighted coins.

Probability distributions can be discrete or continuous, depending on the nature of the trial. Researchers can use the **binomial distribution** to compute probabilities for a process where only one of two possible outcomes may occur on each trial. In other words, when the outcome is "pass" or "fail," the binomial distribution would be useful to the researcher in determining the probability that a particular person or group of people would pass or fail.

Of the continuous distributions, the most commonly used are the **uniform distribution** and the **normal distribution**. In this text, the normal distribution is the most important by far, but keep in mind that there are others.

The *uniform distribution* is useful because it represents variables that are equally distributed over a given interval. For example, if the length of time until the next traffic accident occurs at a particularly busy intersection is equally likely to be any value between one and thirty days, then a researcher could use the uniform distribution to calculate probabilities for the time until the next accident occurs.

The normal distribution is perhaps the most useful probability distribution and is used in a diverse array of applications across many disciplines. There some incredibly useful mathematical probabilities that are associated with the normal distribution, and we will use several of those to our advantage in later sections. The normal distribution is characterized by probabilities (or scores) clustering around the mean or "center" of the distribution. As you move farther and farther from the average, the less probable (frequently) an observation becomes. In our everyday life, we observe that height is normally distributed. If we see a man that is 6' 1" tall, we don't think much of it. If we see a man who is 7' 3" tall, we have to make an effort not to stare. Our six-footer is a little tall, but close enough to the mean that we see people of that height on a fairly regular basis. When we see a seven-footer, we take notice because we encounter men of that height *infrequently*. The same thing can be said for had sizes, ring sizes, shoe sizes and about anything else that is found in nature.

The normal distribution is characterized by the classic bell-shaped curve, and when considering probability distributions, the areas under the curve represent (as you already guessed) *probabilities*.

The normal distribution has many useful statistical properties that make it a popular choice for statistical modeling (often, even when it shouldn't be used). One of these properties is known as *symmetry*, the idea that the probabilities of values below the mean are matched by the probabilities of values that are equally far above the mean. In other words, one half of the curve is the mirror image of the other half.

We will delve deeper into the normal curve later, and what we say about the normal curve in the context of frequency distributions is equally true for probability distributions. The characteristics of the normal curve don't change, regardless of what we are measuring. At this stage, just keep in mind that probability distributions are useful because they let us determine the probability of a particular outcome of a particular experiment *if* the event actually follows the selected distribution.

Also, keep in mind that any curve that can be graphed can also be described by an equation. Those equations can be fed into computer software such as Excel, such that when we "feed-in" a particular score that follows a particular probability distribution, the software can give us back the probability using the equation. Of course, all of the formulas are hidden "under the hood," and we just see a probability magically appear in a cell where we requested it.

Probability Sampling Methods

Probability sampling techniques are the most desirable because they rely on chance to determine the selection of participants in a study. If a sample is chosen by random rules (i.e., it is not systematic), it is highly likely that the sample will be representative of the population. Therefore, researchers should use **probability sampling** methods whenever possible.

*A **probability sampling** method is any sampling method that utilizes randomization for selecting participants.*

Simple Random Samples

The most common type of probability sample is the **simple random sample**. In this procedure, each member of the population has an *equal* and *independent* chance of being selected from the population as part of the sample. Equal and independent are the critical terms.

-The chances are **equal** because there is no bias in the process that would cause one person to be chosen over another.

-The chances are **independent** because the choice of one person does not alter the chance of any other person being selected.

The beauty of this method is that (the vast majority of the time) it results in a sample with characteristics very close to those of the population. That is, it is free of *bias*.

> **Bias** is present in a sample when some members of the population have a greater chance of being selected than other members.

To draw a simple random sample from a population, you need to take four basic steps: First, you must define the population from which you want to select the sample. Second, you need to list all the members of your population. Such a list is referred to as a **frame**. Third, each listed member of the population must have a number assigned to it. Lastly, you use a random criterion to select the sample you want. Traditionally, subjects were selected based on a table of random numbers. (You can find such tables in the back of any statistics text along with instructions for use).

These days, you can use a statistical package for the computer (like SPSS) to randomly select a sample for you. If you do not have the statistical software, you can find random number generators on the internet. You can flip coins, toss dice, draw names from a hat—whatever—so long as the method produces the same chance of being selected for every member of the population.

> Simple random sampling identifies an unbiased sample.

Systematic Sampling

Systematic sampling is easier to do than simple random sampling. The tradeoff is that it is less unbiased because it reduces the chance that certain individuals in the population will be selected. In systematic sampling, every kth name on the list is chosen. (kth is a shorthand used by researchers where k stands for any number you want to put in its place). To find k, all you have to do is divide the number of people in the population by the sample size you want to obtain. To add an element of randomness to the process, most researchers will choose a starting point at random.

Stratified Sampling

The previously discussed methods of sampling are great if specific characteristics of the population are of no concern to the researcher. If, however, the researcher is considering a specific characteristic of the population (such as race, age, gender) that is not equally distributed in the population to begin with, a different sampling technique is in order. **Stratified sampling** allows the researcher to choose a sample that is forced to fit the profile of the population. Stratified sampling is used to ensure that the strata (layers) in the population are closely represented in the sample. Let's say that a political scientist is conducting a study of voting behavior in a particular region where 60% of the voting population is Republican, and 40% is Democrat. It wouldn't make sense to draw a sample that is half Democrat and half Republican—we know from the start that such a sample would not be representative of the population. If we want a sample that accurately reflects the population, we need a sample where 60% of the voting population is Republican, and 40% is Democrat. Stratified sampling allows us to achieve this.

To achieve a stratified sample, you must list each stratum separately. In the above example, we would need to list Democrats and Republicans separately. Let's say we want a sample of 100 subjects. To get such a sample, we would select 60 participants from the Republican list and 40 from the Democrat list. Thus, our sample is stratified just like our population.

Cluster Sampling

The final type of probability sampling that we will discuss is cluster sampling. In a cluster sample, groups are chosen rather than particular individuals. Let's say we are doing a national study on police officer's perceptions of domestic violence. To use the other probability sampling techniques we've already discussed, we'd need to

Adam J. McKee

obtain a list of every police officer in the United States. As far as I know, no such list exists now or is likely to exist in the future (if you know of such a list, please send it to me!) It is entirely possible, however, to obtain a list of every police department in the United States (hard, but you can do it). With cluster sampling, we select a random sample of police departments. The major weakness of this method is that the members of a group may have something in common that contributes to a bias.

Key Terms

Population, Sample, Parameter, Statistic, Probability Sampling, Simple Random Sample, Bias, Sampling Frame, Systematic Sampling, Stratified Sampling, Cluster Sampling

Section 2.2:
Nonprobability Sampling

n this general category of sampling techniques, the common thread is that the probability of selecting a particular individual from the population is not known. This violates the basic assumption of probability samples that each individual has an equal and independent chance of being selected.

> *A Nonprobability sample is a sample drawn by a method that does not use randomization as a component of selecting participants.*

Convenience Sampling

Convenience sampling is just what the name implies. You used the sample because the individuals were convenient—easy to rope in. This type of sample is sadly common among academic researchers. College students are often used as research subjects because professors conducting research can lure them in with promises of extra credit. If your population of interest is college students, then that may be okay. In general, this is a terrible sampling method and should be used with extreme caution.

> *Samples of convenience are biased.*

Quota Sampling

Some research projects will require that you have a stratified sample, but you cannot obtain a probability sample for some reason. Let's say that you are conducting a study on drug use, education, and recidivism. It would be difficult indeed to get a list of the population of cocaine using convicts that hold Master's degrees. A situation like this suggests quota sampling. First, you have to identify how many people you need in the sample with those characteristics. Then, you search everywhere for people that meet the criteria. Once you reach the number that you wanted, you simply stop. You have your sample.

Sampling Error

Whenever a sample is drawn, only that part of the population that is included (by definition!) in the sample is measured. The idea is to use the sample to represent the entire population. Because of this, there will always be some error in the data, resulting from those members of the population who were not measured. This discrepancy between what we observe in the sample and what is true in the population is known as **sampling error**.

Random sampling procedures always result in some degree of sampling error.

The more people we include (the larger our sample is), the more accurately the sample will reflect the population, and the less sampling error we will have. If a census is performed (a 100 percent sample is a census), there will be no sampling error.

Selecting a large sample size does not correct for errors due to bias.

When newspapers print things like "the **margin of error** is plus or minus three percent," it seems to suggest that the results are accurate to within the stated percentage. This view of it is completely wrong and grossly misleading. That is not to say anything bad about the media; they merely want to warn people about sampling error. However, most readers are not trained in statistical methods and may fail to assume that all surveys—all data coming from samples—are estimates. *Estimates may be wrong.*

Let us take a public opinion poll with a 4% margin of error as an example. (We use percentages in this example because they are very easy in intuitive in interpretation. Keep in mind that these basic ideas apply to *any* statistic computed from a sample). If we continue to take random samples from the population 100 times, then the results would fall within that confidence interval 95% the time. That means that if you asked a question from this poll 100 times, 95 of those times the percentage of people giving a particular answer would be within 4 points of the percentage who gave that same answer in this poll. Why only 95% of the time? In reality, the margin of error is what statisticians call a **confidence interval**. The math behind it is much like the math behind the standard deviation.

Key Terms

Nonprobability Sampling, Convenience Sampling, Quota Sampling, Margin of Error, Confidence Interval

Section 2.3:
Describing Data

Recall from previous chapters that the essence of empirical research is *observation*. Because science is also systematic, these observations are recorded, often in the form of measurements. As we have already seen, these measurements often result in masses of numbers. Therefore, the researcher will usually end up what a mass of data that is essentially meaningless. It is meaningless because it is overwhelming—the average mind simply cannot wrap itself around page after page of numbers. Before data can become useful, it must be simplified and organized.

Variables

The type of data that you have determines the type of statistical procedure that you will use to describe it. Review the types of variables presented in the section of *Variables*. As we proceed to discuss statistics that describe a set of data, it is important to understand what statistics are appropriate for what type of data. For example, we cannot compute the mean of Democrat, Republican, or Other. It makes no sense!

Distributions of Data

A set of scores that have been organized lowest to highest is referred to as a **distribution**. To adequately describe a distribution of data, a researcher needs to report three things:

1. A measure of central tendency

2. A measure of variability

3. A description of shape

Given these three things, we know a great deal about a distribution of data. We will consider each of these ideas briefly in this section, then we will treat them in greater detail in their own sections later on.

A distribution is a set of scores that have been organized from lowest to highest.

Generally, a set of scores is entered into a table. These days, the table is usually a computer **spreadsheet**. These can be generic spreadsheet programs (like Excel), or specialized statistical packages (like SPSS). Cases (data for each subject) run in rows across the page and variables run in columns up and down the page. Such a rectangular organization of data is called a **matrix**. A professor's grade book is a good example.

Figure 2

	C13		f_x	=AVERAGE(C6:C12)	
	A	B	C	D	E	F
1						
2						
3			Statistics Grade Book			
4						
5		Name	Test 1	Test 2	Test 3	Final Exam
6		Bob	76	79	81	78
7		Joe	83	85	80	82
8		Suzie	92	98	90	92
9		Linda	77	73	70	72
10		James	65	69	66	67
11		Victoria	56	72	71	70
12		Edward	98	94	92	91
13		Average:	78	81	79	79
14						

Notice in the figure above how the data are arranged in an Excel spreadsheet. For each student (subject) there is a row of information that contains the student's name and scores for three exams and a final exam. Each of those exams can be considered a variable because the value changes from person to person. The bottom line provides the average (mean) of each test. In this example, it makes sense to call each test result a score. Note, however, that individual data points (**cells**) are often referred to as scores regardless of whether the data represents a test. Researchers speak of "scores" on opinion data and anything else that they have measured.

Note that the term *data* is plural and you must use the appropriate verb form when writing about your analysis. The singular form is *datum*, but the term is seldom seen.

Measures of Central Tendency

What is the typical salary? What is the IQ score of the average Joe? About how well educated are most American voters? These common types of questions are questions about the center of a distribution of scores. When we ask them, we want a single number that summarizes where most people fall on a given scale. Measures of center answer this question because most people are average. That is, most people fall around the average on any given scale. The more extreme a score is, the less likely it is to occur and the farther away from them mean it is.

We will consider three major measures of central tendency in this text:

1. Mean

2. Median

3. Mode

These three measures are appropriate for data measured at different levels and are only accurate as measures of center under certain conditions. We will consider each in turn in a later section. For now, we will simply describe them.

The *mean* is what we usually mean when we talk about an average. The **mean** is the sum of the scores divided by the number of scores. The **median** is the middlemost score in a distribution of scores. The median is most often used where there are extreme scores in the distribution that would unduly influence the mean. The **mode** is the most frequently occurring value in a distribution.

Measures of Variability

Knowing the center of a distribution gives us a partial picture of the characteristics of a set of scores, but that picture is often not in clear focus. In other words, a measure of central tendency, standing alone, can lead us to an inaccurate view of the characteristics of a distribution.

Let us take the weather report as an example. Suppose the weather report tells you that the average temperature tomorrow will be 70 degrees. That sounds comfortable, so you decide to wear jeans and a t-shirt. Little do you know that the low will be a chilly 45 degrees and that the high will be a sunny 95 degrees. The problem is that you did not take in to account how much the temperature at any given time would *deviate* from the mean. This potential confusion is why weather reports usually report the high and low temperature. When it comes to weather, we care about extreme scores more than we do the middle. For most social science variables, we also want to consider how far scores are spread out from the middle.

Social science researchers often refer to the high and low scores as the minimum and maximum. Reporting the minimum score and the maximum score is an elementary approach to reporting the variability of a distribution of scores.

Four other measures of spread will be discussed in this text:

1. The range
2. The interquartile range (IQR)
3. Standard deviation
4. Variance

Synonyms of Variability

The idea of variability among a set of scores is very important in statistics. There are several terms that researchers use to talk about variability. Spread, Dispersion, Variability, and Deviation are commonly used. Your author likes the homemade word **Spreadoutness**.

Shapes of Distributions

Once a set of raw scores has been organized into a tabular distribution, we can consider the *shape* of the distribution. The most common way to accomplish this visually is to graph it with the scores along the horizontal axis and the frequencies (*f*) along the vertical axis. The result is formally known as a frequency polygon, and more commonly as a line graph. When the number of cases is very large, the polygon will tend to take on a smooth shape that is often referred to as a **curve**.

The most important shape of any distribution in statistics is the *normal curve*. This curve, illustrated below, is also called the *bell curve* because of its resemblance to a bell. This curve is often found in nature. That is, the majority of cases tend to cluster around the mean, and become increasingly rare the farther you get from the mean. It is easy to find a man who wears a size 10 shoe because that is about average. You will have a much more difficult time finding a man who wears a size six shoe, as you will with a man that wears a size sixteen shoe. The normal curve is also very important because its properties allow us to do inferential statistics, a topic that we will cover in later sections.

Figure 3.   A Normal Distribution.

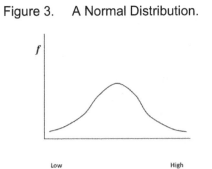

Some distributions are not normal. That is, they do not have the characteristic bell shape. It is possible for scores to cluster at one extreme (high or low) rather than in the middle. Such distributions are said to be **skewed**.

*A distribution is said to be **skewed** when scores cluster to the left or right rather than the center.*

When scores cluster on the low end and the tale is longer to the right, the curve is said to be **positively skewed**. When scores cluster on the high end and the tail is longer to the left, the curve is said to be **negatively skewed**. Positive and negative refer to which end of the number line the long tail points. The Histogram in the figure below shows a frequency distribution of a set of test scores. The curve overlaid on the histogram is a normal one. We can tell by how well that the histogram matches the normal curve that our test scores are normally distributed.

Figure 4.   A Normally Distributed Set of Test Scores.

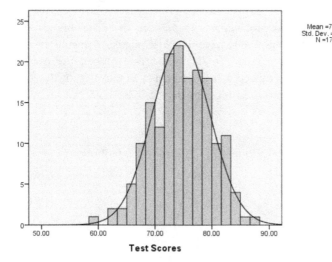

A more precise way to determine the skewness of a set of scores is to examine a **skewness statistic**. The skewness statistic takes on both positive and negative values. If the skewness is positive, then the data are positively skewed. If the skewness statistic is negative, the data are negatively skewed. If the skewness statistic is equal to zero, then the curve is perfectly symmetrical. Note that a perfectly symmetrical curve almost never happens with real data. There will be some slight deviation from symmetry. In interpreting the skewness statistic, many researchers consider any value over 1 to be extremely skewed, any value between 0.5 and 1 to be moderately skewed, and any value below 0.5 to be approximately symmetrical.

Figure 5.   A Skewed Distribution.

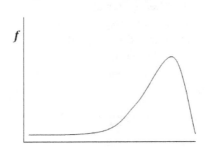

Another potential problem has to do with the distribution's central peak. A normal curve, it is expected to have the "bell" shape. Some distributions will be tall and pointed, and some will be flat and broad. When the central peak of the distribution is not as expected, it is referred to as **kurtosis**. If the distribution is tall and peaked, it is known as **mesokurtic**. If it is short and broad, it is known as **platykurtic**.

Figure 6.   A Peaked Distribution.

Like the skewness statistic, a normal distribution has a kurtosis statistic of zero. Positive kurtosis values indicate that the observations cluster more, making the distribution peaked (mesokurtic).   Negative kurtosis values indicate that the observations cluster less and have shorter tails (platykurtic).

Distributions that have two peaks are known as **bimodal distributions**.   Note that this does not mean that the data have two values that tied exactly for the mode (the most frequently occurring value). The points do not have to be exactly equal in height. The term *bimodal* is used less precisely to describe a distribution that has two obvious high points.

Computing Descriptive Statistics in Excel

For many descriptive statistics, Excel provides individual functions to calculate them. If you want to produce several descriptive statistics at the same time, it is easier to use the *Descriptive Statistics Tool* in the *Analysis ToolPak*. The ToolPak is a set of automated tools that allow you to conduct statistical analyses that would otherwise be tedious or not available with regular Excel functions. It is an add-in, so you need to load the ToolPak the first time you use it.

Figure 7. Descriptive Statistics in Excel.

	A	B	C	D	E	F	G	H	I
		I18				f_x			
1									
2									
3				Statistics Grade Book				Test 1	
4									
5		Name	Test 1	Test 2	Test 3	Final Exam		Mean	78.14286
6		Bob	76	79	81	78		Standard Error	5.518059
7		Joe	83	85	80	82		Median	77
8		Suzie	92	98	90	92		Mode	#N/A
9		Linda	77	73	70	72		Standard Deviation	14.59941
10		James	65	69	66	67		Sample Variance	213.1429
11		Victoria	56	72	71	70		Kurtosis	-0.64225
12		Edward	98	94	92	91		Skewness	-0.18994
13		**Average:**	78	81	79	79		Range	42
14								Minimum	56
15								Maximum	98
16								Sum	547
17								Count	7
18									

Figure 7 above shows the results of running the Descriptive Statistics Tool on Test 1 of the hypothetical statistics grade book data. So far, most of these statistics will be unknown to you. You should, however, notice that the "mean" reported in the Test 1 table is the same as the "average" reported at the bottom of the Test 1 column of the grade book. The "sum" in the Test 1 table is ΣX, which means all the scores (for Test 1) added up. The "count" is the number of cases (subjects) which we will symbolize as n.

Loading the Analysis ToolPak in Excel

1. Click on the **Microsoft Office Button**, then select **Excel Options**.
2. Click **Add-ins**, and then the **Manage Box**, then select **Excel Add-ins**.
3. Click on **Go**.
4. Find the **Add-ins Available Box**, then select the **Analysis ToolPak** and then click **OK**.

Note: After you load the Analysis ToolPak, the Data analysis command is available in the Analysis group under the Data Tab.

Key Terms

Distribution, Normal Curve, Symmetrical, Skewness, Positive Skew, Negative Skew, Kurtosis, Platykurtic, Mesokurtic, Bimodal Distribution, Matrix, Spreadsheet, Cell, Data/Datum, Measures of Central Tendency, Mean, Median, Mode, Measures of Variability, Range, Interquartile Range, Variance, Standard Deviation, Skewness Statistic

Section 2.4:
Percentages & Rates

The term **percent** means *per one hundred*. You can think of a percentage as a special fraction that always has 100 in the denominator. For example, if males make up 49% of the population, then 49 out of every 100 people will be male. Any fraction can be converted to a percentage. This is very useful because it facilitates comparisons of things that would otherwise be hard to compare because they have different frequencies.

For example, a criminologist wanting to compare homicides in rural areas versus urban areas would not be able to use the actual number of homicides because there are far fewer people in rural areas, so homicides would be far more infrequent in those rural areas. By using percentages (or rates), the criminologist has a better method of comparing Monticello, Arkansas (population 10,000) with New York City.

Computing a Percentage

To compute a percentage, simply divide the part by the whole and multiply the result by 100. For example, if 7 out of 113 convicted house burglars report carrying a firearm while committing their crime, the 6.2% reported carrying firearms in the commission of burglaries (7/113 = .062 x 100 = 6.2%).

A **proportion** is a part of one. We compute a proportion following the same procedure we use to compute a percent, but we do not multiply the decimal number by 100. That is, a proportion is a fractional part of a whole where the whole is always equal to one. For example, a proportion of .50 is the same as saying 50% or the fraction ½. Proportions are rarely ever reported in the popular press because the average person without benefit of statistical training does not understand them. Percentages are preferred. Social scientists reporting research results in professional journals are far more likely to report findings as proportions.

Rates

In some research situations, we are interested in characteristics that are very rare. In such cases, percentages can be awkward to read and difficult to interpret. We can apply the same logic of using a percentage to a larger number than 100. If a percentage, being a **rate** per 100, provides a number that is too small, then we can consider the rate per a larger number than 100. For example, the FBI uses the rate per 100,000 to report the occurrences of crime in the United States.

Computing a Rate from a Percentage	
To convert from a percentage to this rate:	Multiply the percentage by this number:
Per 1,000	10
Per 10,000	100
Per 100,000	1,000
Per 1,000,000	10,000

You can use the same logic in reverse to convert some other rate to a percentage. To do this, you will divide rather than multiply.

Computing a Percentage from a Rate	
To convert from this rate to a percentage:	Divide the rate by this number:
Per 1,000	10
Per 10,000	100
Per 100,000	1,000
Per 1,000,000	10,000

Cumulative Percent and Percentile Rank

A **cumulative percentage** indicates the percentage of scores at and below a given score. A cumulative percentage is also known as a **percentile rank**. Most every college student is familiar with percentile ranks because they have been given their percentile rank on standardized college admission tests. If you scored in the 87th Percentile on the SAT, that means that 87% of the students taking the test when you did had the same or a lower score than you did.

Note that the Quartiles are also percentiles in multiples of 25%. That is, the First Quartile is also the 25th percentile, and the Second Quartile is also the 50th Percentile, and the Third Quartile is the 75th Percentile.

Key Terms

Percentage, Proportion, Rate, Cumulative Percent, Percentile Rank

Section 2.5:
Frequency Distributions

A *frequency distribution* is used to organize and summarize data. Remember that **frequency** means the number of times something happens, and its symbol is *f*. The symbol *N*, the number of subjects, is also used to stand for frequency.

A **frequency distribution** is simply a table that tells us how many things were observed in a particular category. The most common way to present a frequency distribution is to have the scores (or categories) listed in order from highest to lowest in the first column, and the number of cases listed in the second column. Many researchers also include the percentage of cases associated with each score.

Frequency distributions fall under the heading of descriptive statistics. Recall that the purpose of descriptive statistics is to organize and summarize data. Constructing a frequency distribution does both. Because all of the possible values of a variable are collapsed into categories with the number of scores that fell into that category, the frequency distribution has the potential to reduce a very large, incomprehensible matrix of data into something that can be seen and interpreted at a glance.

It is common to present frequency distributions as both tables and graphs. Either way, two things are presented to the reader. The first is a list of the categories that the variable has been divided into. Also, the table or graph presents the number of people that fell into each of the categories. A very simple frequency distribution may involve the variable *gender*. A table would provide a column with male and female in it, and another column that has the number of males and the number of females. A histogram would have a bar showing the number of males, and another bar showing the number of males.

Since the scores (or categories) are ordered, a frequency distribution shows how scores are distributed on a scale; that's where the name comes from. It is a matter of custom that the scores be listed from highest to lowest. Most computer programs, such as Microsoft's Excel, will sort data from least to greatest (ascending), or greatest to least (descending).

When presented with a frequency distribution table, you can determine several other descriptive statistics. To determine the number of participants in the entire study, add up the frequency for every category ($\Sigma f = N$). To determine the sum of the scores, take each **X** (score category) value and multiply it by its frequency, then sum those products (note that this does not work for categories that are a range of scores).

Proportions and Percentages

You can easily obtain the proportion or percentage of study participants that fall into a particular category in a frequency distribution. To obtain the proportion, divide the frequency of the category you are interested in by the total number of people in the study (proportion = f/N). The proportion associated with each category is called its *relative frequency*. Recall that while proportions can be expressed as fractions, it is more common to see them expressed in decimal form. To determine the percentage of participants that fall into a particular category, compute the proportion of people that fall into the category you are interested in and multiply that by 100. These percentages are often shown in frequency distributions by adding a column headed with the percent sign (%).

Grouped Frequency Distributions

Recall the purpose of a frequency distribution is to summarize a set of data. We will fail at this purpose if the table contains too many categories. For this reason, continuous data are often organized into logical intervals and then listing the intervals in the table rather than each specific score. For example, a professor wanting to summarize students' scores on a test could list each possible score from 0 to 100. This would likely produce a table larger than the actual column of raw scores. Since letter grades are assigned in ten point intervals, it would be logical to establish intervals that capture the lowest score and then proceed by increments of 10% until the highest score is captured. These groups of scores, or intervals, are often called *class intervals*.

If you are constructing a grouped frequency distribution table, examine the data as we did above to see if there is a logical number of categories to use. If no clear "natural" classification emerges, then construct your table with ten categories. Of course, you will want to adjust this number if ten categories result in an illogical presentation. Your ultimate goal is to present your data in a form that is easy to understand. It is best to make all of your intervals the same width. This advice is commonly ignored with a "catch all" category at the end of the list. Tables with much larger intervals in the final category can be misleading because that category because it is much broader than the other, may have the higher frequency. Consider this when you are the consumer of research.

The primary advantage of presenting data as a grouped frequency distribution is that it is easy to "see" the characteristics of the data at a glance. Remember, when you group data you are necessarily losing information.

Computing a Frequency Distribution in Excel

To compute a frequency distribution in Excel, use the FREQUENCY function. Note that this function returns an array.

Arrays In Excel

For some reason, you cannot just click "OK" to exit the Insert Function dialog box. You must do so by pressing CTRL+SHIFT+ENTER at the same time.

Figure 8

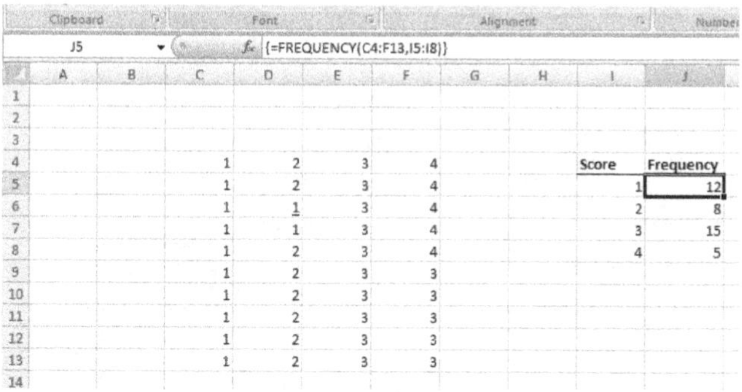

Histograms

A **histogram** is a graph that has vertical bars indicating the frequency, rate, or percentage of different categories or points along a continuous variable. By convention, the frequency is placed along the vertical edge of the graph, and the category is placed along the horizontal line at the bottom. You can use a histogram with either quantitative or qualitative data. The basic idea is to show how a variable is distributed among different categories. The *mode* of a histogram is the most frequently occurring score. A distribution of scores with two such high points is referred to as **bimodal**.

Creating a Histogram in Excel

First, you will need to create a frequency table that lists the category headings, and a corresponding column that contains the frequencies for each category. For example, let us say a political scientist is interested in political party preferences for a local election.

Figure 9. Frequency Tables in Excel.

D8			f_x	=SUM(D4:D7)	
	A	B	C	D	E
1					
2			**Party Preference**		
3					
4			Republican	100	
5			Democrat	87	
6			Independent	36	
7			Undecided	12	
8			N =	235	
9					

Next, you will highlight both the labels and the frequencies. Under the **Insert** tab, find **charts** and select **column**. For a traditional look, select the simple two-dimensional chart listed first. Once the graph is generated, you can right click on it and edit the legend.

Figure 10. Histograms in Excel.

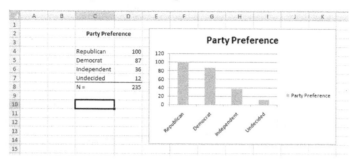

Once you have your chart formatted as you want it, you can right-click on it, select copy, and then paste it into a word document. This is how you would present your chart in a research report.

Note that **pie charts** can be used to illustrate similar data to bar charts. When the number of levels of the variable is small, pie charts may work just as well or better in getting your information across. In other words, you can use a pie chart with quantitative or qualitative data to show the distribution of the data among different categories. For example, suppose that Bob is a raving fan of Community Coffee and starts a café based on selling their products. He wants to analyze the café's sales by coffee style. The styles that Bob sells are French Roast, Breakfast Blend, Dark Roast, and Café Special. By creating a pie chart, Bob can show potential investors what styles are being sold, and what proportion of sales each makes up at the same time.

Outliers

An **outlier** is simply a score in a distribution of scores that is far away from the other scores in magnitude. If we were to establish a frequency distribution of household income, then the score for Bill Gates would be an outlier because Mr. Gates has a shockingly large income compared to the average person. Outliers are commonly defined as scores that fall more than three standard deviation units either side of the mean (we will discuss standard deviation in a later section).

Outliers and Skew

A distribution is said to be **skewed** if it has outliers at one end and not the other. That is, scores tend to "lean" toward one side of the distribution. When the outliers are on the right, the distribution is said to have a *positive skew*. When the outliers are on the left, the distribution is said to have a *negative skew*.

Line Graph

A *line graph* servers a similar function to the histogram. When we graph frequencies, we can generate what is called a **frequency polygon**. Don't let that "polygon" stuff throw you off. All we are talking about is a line graph that shows frequencies. If there is a good point to having that name, it is that we are reminded we are dealing with frequencies. We'll be spending a lot of time talking about frequency polygons later. For now, just keep in mind that the height of the line (the vertical axis) tells us the frequency, and the position left to right along the horizontal axis (think of this one as a number line) tells us the score. Since most people tend to be average (unless you ask them), we find that the curve is highest in the middle where the mean is, and it trails off quickly to either side of the mean. Not every curve takes on this bell (think Liberty Bell) shape, but many things in nature do. The mathematical properties of the normal curve allow us to do some pretty cool things that make us look really smart. More on that later.

Generating a Line Graph in Excel

To generate a line graph of frequencies in excel, you will need a frequency distribution table with the column headings in one column and the frequency counts in the other. To generate the graph, simply highlight both columns. Then, under the **Insert** tab, find **Charts** then choose **Line**. For the most traditional looking line graph, choose the first two-dimensional style under the available options.

Figure 11. Line Graph in Excel.

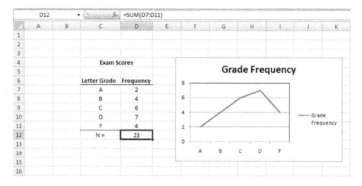

Don't get stuck in a rut of thinking that line graphs *always* measure frequency. This is extremely common in the social and behavioral sciences and will be the most common use in this text. In business, however, the most common line graphs are those that show changes in price over *time*. For "stock charts" and other types of price information, the height of the line will tell you the price, and the placement of the "dot" on the horizontal axis shows the time at which the security was trading at that price. As every stock trader knows, it is critical to understand *what* is being measured and *how* it is being measured when interpreting a line graph. Stock traders can view price changes by the minute, in 5-minute increments, in day-long increments, week-long increments, month-long increments, and quarterly increments. Using the wrong interpretation of a stock chart can lead to a financial disaster, just as making practice decisions on a faulty interpretation of a graph can lead to disaster for the social scientist.

The reason the financial world likes this type of chart so much is that it allows one to easily spot trends. With a line graph, it is easy to see patterns in a data set. For example, a Wall Streeter can tell with a glance at a price chart that the price of Microsoft stock rose steadily throughout April into mid-May before falling back in late May and then recovering somewhat by the end of the month. With the stock in an "uptrend," the trader may decide that Microsoft is likely to go higher in the coming weeks. In other words, these types of graphs may be used by investors to identify which assets are likely to rise in the future based on their past performance—or at least a lot of investors *think* it works that way.

Key Terms

Frequency, f, n, Outlier, Skewness, Line Graph

Chapter 3:
Describing Variables

Adam J. McKee

Section 3.1:
Measures of Central Tendency

Measures of central tendency provide a single number that typifies the average score. The most commonly reported of these are the *mean*, the *median*, and the *mode*. The most popular among these is the mean. The mean is so popular, in fact, that it is often simply called the *average*. We will treat the term *mean* as referring to a specific statistic, and the term *average* as a more general term that is synonymous with *measures of central tendency*. To identify the center of a data set, then, you use measures that are known as measures of central tendency; the most important of these are the *mean*, *median*, and *mode*. The mean represents the *average* (and in business—and Excel—means the exact same thing) value in a data set, while the median represents the *midpoint*. The median is a value that separates the data into two equal halves; half (exactly 50%) of the elements in the data set are less than the median, and the remaining half (the other 50%) are greater than the median. The mode is the most *commonly occurring* value in the data set.

Mean

The **mean** (symbolized X and sometimes M as a sample statistic, or μ as a population parameter) is the average that is the "balance point" in a distribution. It is calculated by adding up (summing) all of the scores and dividing by the number of scores (n). The mean provides researchers with a way of finding the most typical value in a set of scores.

64

Computing the Mean

Compute the mean using the following formula:

$$\overline{X} = \frac{\Sigma X}{N}$$

Where:

- $\overline{X}$ is the mean of X
- ΣX is the sum of the X values
- And N is the number of elements

In a skewed distribution, the mean will be "pulled" toward the outliers. That is, the mean is sensitive to extreme scores. The more extreme the outliers are, the less useful the mean is as a measure of central tendency. When extreme scores will influence the mean too much, it should be abandoned in favor of a statistic that does not use every value in the distribution and thus is not biased by extreme scores.

The mean is the most widely used measure of central tendency, but it can give deceptive results if the data contain any unusually large or small values, known as outliers.

An important characteristic of the mean is that it is the "balance point" of the distribution. This means that it is the point at which the differences between every other score and the mean sum to zero. This may not seem very important now, but the importance of it will be more important later when we discuss measures of variability such as the standard deviation and variance.

The mean is an appropriate measure of central tendency when:

- The data are measured at the interval or ratio level

- The data are approximately normally distributed

Computing the Mean in Excel

To compute the mean of a set of scores in Excel, use the **AVERAGE** function.

Figure 12. Average Function in Excel.

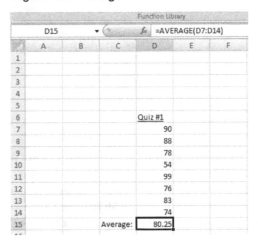

Median

The **median** is the average that indicates the value below which half the cases lie. That is, the median is the point at which 50% of the values fall above and 50% fall below. It is the middle point of the distribution. The median has to do with how many scores there are in a distribution, and is not affected by the value of those scores. This means that the median is not sensitive to extreme scores as the mean is. There is no special symbol used for the Median, it is usually written out or abbreviated *Mdn*.

Computing the Median

There is no formula for the median. It is determined by taking the following steps:

1. Arrange the scores in order from low to high
2. If there are an odd number of scores, the median is the middle most number in the list
3. If there are an even number of scores, obtain the median by computing the mean of the two middle most scores

Computing the Median in Excel

To compute the Median in Excel, use the **MEDIAN** function. It is formatted just like the AVERAGE function, which returns the mean.

Figure 13

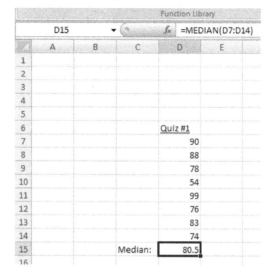

Since the mean median is not very sensitive to extreme scores, it is the preferred method of measuring central tendency when we know such scores are present. For example, *median household income* is usually reported by the Bureau of the Census instead of mean household income. This is because mean household income is overstated by the presence of a relatively small number of extremely wealthy households. As a result, median household income is thought to be a superior measure of how standards of living are changing over time.

Mode

The **mode** is the most frequently occurring score in a distribution. The mode is especially useful in describing nominal level data. Nominal level data names something. In other words, the mode can be used for either quantitative or qualitative data. If you were researching peoples' favorite color, for example, and more people selected blue than any other color, then blue would be the mode.

Computing the Mode

There is no formula for the mode. To obtain the mode, simply order the scores from low to high and select the number with the highest frequency.

Computing the Mode in Excel

Let's say that a researcher is interested in the most frequent political party affiliation of his survey respondents. He has coded Democrat = 1, Republican = 2, and Independent = 3. To find the mode, use the **MODE** function.

Figure 14. The Mode in Excel.

Clipboard			Font		
	C20	▼	f_x	=MODE(C4:C18)	
	A	B	C	D	E
1					
2					
3		ID	Party		
4		1	1		
5		2	2		
6		3	3		
7		4	3		
8		5	2		
9		6	1		
10		7	1		
11		8	2		
12		9	3		
13		10	1		
14		11	2		
15		12	2		
16		13	3		
17		14	1		
18		15	2		
19					
20		Mode:	2		

Selecting a Measure of Central Tendency

Selecting a measure of central tendency is not a difficult task if you keep the following points in mind:

-If possible, choose the mean. This is because it is useful when paired with more advanced statistics that we will discuss in later sections.

-If the distribution is not symmetrical (is skewed by extreme scores) choose the median.

-If the data are nominal, choose the mode.

Key Terms

Measure of Central Tendency, Mean, Median, Mode

Important Symbols

$$\overline{X}, \sum X, n$$

Section 3.2:
Measures of Variability

Variability is also referred to as *dispersion* or *spread*. These terms all refer to differences among scores. These differences indicate how subjects vary. Measures of dispersion (a synonym of variability) identify how "spread out" a data set is, relative to the center. This provides a way of determining if the members of a data set tend to be very close to each other or if they tend to be widely scattered. In other words, how much does each subject's score differ from the average? In most research reports, you will find a measure of variability reported along with a measure of central tendency. These two statistics, along with a discussion of shape, adequately describe a distribution of scores. The amount of variation in a group of scores is important for both statistical and practical reasons. Simply put, a measure of center often does not tell the whole story.

For example, according to the Bureau of the Census, the median household income for the United States is $50,233.00. That makes it sound like most Americans are all doing pretty well. If we just look that the median (a measure of center), we miss the fact that poverty is still a big problem in the United States. We would not know that about 15% of Americans live in poverty. We would not know that around 27% of single-parent families live in poverty. We would not know that a much larger proportion of minorities live in poverty than whites. These problems with observing only a measure of center arise because individuals tend to vary widely from the center. To get an idea of the larger picture, we have to look at the center, but we must also consider variability.

The more variable a group's scores, the more **heterogeneous** *the group is. Conversely, the smaller the variation, the more* **homogenous** *the group is.*

Range and Interquartile Range

This simplest measure of variability is the distance between the lowest score and the highest score in a set of data, also known as the **range**. Some researchers simply report the highest and lowest value as the range; others subtract the lowest score from the highest score to give a range statistic. Thus we can interpret the range statistic is the maximum possible difference between scores in a set of data. The larger the value of the range statistic, the more variability there is in the set of scores.

A critical weakness of the range statistic is that it is based on two (often extreme) scores and may not reflect the true variability of the distribution. In other words, it reflects the maximum variability within the distribution, and not the average variability.

Computing the Range

Range = Maximum Score – Minimum Score

The **interquartile range** (IQR) indicates the scores obtained by the middle 50% of participants. That is, we ignore the lowest 25% and the highest 25%. This middle section supplies us with a measure of variability that is resistant to the effects of extreme scores at either end. To determine the interquartile range, you must first identify the 25th percentile and the 75th percentile. A critical weakness of the IQR is that it is based on only half of your data. When it is computed, potentially valuable information is thrown away.

Computing the Interquartile Range

To obtain the Interquartile Range, follow these steps:

1. Order the scores from low to high.

2. Identify the median of the distribution (middle most score), and mark the scores below the median as a group and the scores above the median as a group.

3. Find the median of the lower half of the scores: That is the 25th Percentile.

4. Find the median of the upper half of the scores: that is the 75th Percentile.

5. Subtract the value of the score at the 25th Percentile from the value of the score at the 75th Percentile to obtain the Interquartile Range.

Note that certain measures of variability are commonly reported with certain measures of central tendency because they have similar restrictions as to which type of data with which they are appropriate. The interquartile range is most often reported with the median. Both are insensitive to extreme scores and work well with skewed distributions.

Computing the Quartiles in Excel

To provide the interquartile range, you must compute the values that divide the data into fourths. This can be done easily in Excel using the **QUARTILE** function.

Figure 15

	ID	GPA			Percentile		Quartile	Score
	1	3.87			88.80%		1	3.38
	2	2.97			0.00%		2	3.52
	3	3.23			11.10%		3	3.6575
	4	3.36			22.20%		4	3.93
	5	3.44			33.30%			
	6	3.49			44.40%			
	7	3.55			55.50%			
	8	3.62			66.60%			
	9	3.67			77.70%			
	10	3.93			100.00%			

Formula bar: I6 =QUARTILE(D6:D15,H6)

The QUARTILE function has two arguments. "Array" is the list of scores (GPA in our example) and "Quart" is the number corresponding to the quartile that you want returned, either 1, 2, 3, or 4. Note that the function does not return an array, but a single quartile. To get all four quartiles, you need to set up four functions.

Variance and Standard Deviation

One way to examine variability is to consider how far each score deviates from the mean. On an individual basis, this makes intuitive sense. For example, let us say that you have recently taken a statistics quiz. You find out that you made a score of 50%, and feel absolutely awful about your score. It may help your feelings to learn that the class average was 40%. While not a good score, it is higher than the average score of your classmates by 10%. In this example, the difference between your score and the class average is known as a **deviation score** (*D*).

If we compute a deviation score for every member of the class, we can examine how spread out each person's score is from the mean. The problem with examining deviation scores is that there are as many deviation scores as there are raw scores. As the size of the class (or sample) grows, the harder it is to wrap our minds around what the data is telling us. We can summarize the deviation scores just like we did the raw scores: we can compute an average deviation score. The average of the deviations will provide us with a single number that summarizes the "spreadoutness" of all the scores.

For mathematical reasons, we have to do a few extra steps to get where we want to be with this idea of computing an average deviation score. When we do this, the result is a statistic known as the **standard deviation**. This little statistic is so important that we will spend more time on it later on. For now, just remember that the standard deviation is simply the average distance of the individual scores from the mean of the group. In the next section, we will describe the standard deviation in detail, as well as a closely related statistic known as the **variance**.

Let's review what we've said so far: The standard deviation is the square root of the variance, and is more commonly used than the variance since the variance is expressed in *squared* units. For example, the variance of a series of tuition prices is measured in *squared dollars*, which is nearly impossible to interpret. The corresponding standard deviation is measured in dollars, which is much easier to intuitively grasp.

In statistics, especially when your audience is not composed of social scientists, you should present the most intuitive statistics possible.

Standard deviation and variance are typically superior to some other measures of dispersion, such as the range. The range is the difference between the largest and smallest components in a data set. The range suffers from the disadvantage that it is based on only two scores, so it does not measure the spreadoutness among the leftover values.

Volatility

Different academic disciplines have a habit of calling the same thing by different names. In finance, the spreadoutness of an investment's returns over a specific period of time is called its **volatility**. Investors often use this as a measure of how risky it is to own a particular stock. This is nothing more than the standard deviation that we've already learned about. It makes sense that investors would worry about the standard deviation of stock prices; the size of the average move from the mean tells the investor how much the stock is likely to go up or down (most of the time). Volatility is usually computed on the returns of a particular investment. Returns are the money gained expressed as a percentage. Since the base number is a percentage, volatility is expressed as a percentage as well.

It is important to note that the *returns of investments are not normally distributed*. In coming sections, we will learn a lot of useful rules about what percentage of observations fall within a certain distance of the mean, and we will measure those distances in standard deviations. These rules only work when the measurements we are dealing with are normally distributed. Stock market returns have "fat tails," and don't always perform as our rules suggest. Many investors have been ruined because they didn't take those "fat tails" into account when determining how much risk they were taking on.

Key Terms

Measures of Variability, Spread, Dispersion, Heterogeneous, Homogenous, Range, Interquartile Range, Standard Deviation, Variance

Section 3.3:
Standard Deviation

The *standard deviation* (*s* or *SD*) is the average spread of a group of scores from the mean of the distribution of scores. That is, it is a measure of the rise and fall of scores around the mean. Coupled with the mean, the standard deviation is the most commonly reported measure of variability.

Computing the Standard Deviation

The standard deviation of a sample can be computed using the following equation:

$$s = \sqrt{\frac{\sum (X - \bar{X})^2}{N - 1}}$$

- Where *s* is the standard deviation
- $X - \bar{X}$ is the deviation score
- N is the number of elements in the sample

To apply the formula, you will need to take the following step:

1. Prepare a table with the first column being the scores (*X*)
2. In the cell just below the list of scores, compute the sum of the scores (ΣX)
3. Establish the number of elements in the sample (N)
4. Compute the mean ($\bar{X}$)
5. Create a second column of *Deviation Scores*, where you subtract the mean from each score $(x - \bar{x})$
5. Create a third column where you square the deviation scores $(X - \bar{X})^2$

6. In the cell just below the deviation scores, compute the sum $\sum(X - \bar{X})^2$

7. Compute the degrees of freedom (N-1)

8. Divide the sum of the squared deviation scores by the degrees of freedom to get the *variance* (s^2)

9. Take the square root of the variance to get the standard deviation (s)

Computing Standard Deviation in Excel

To compute the standard deviation of a set of scores in Excel, use the **STDEV** function.

Figure 16.

Clipboard			Font	
C20		▾	f_x =STDEV(C4:C18)	
	A	B	C	D	E
1					
2					
3		ID	IQ		
4		1	90		
5		2	78		
6		3	98		
7		4	111		
8		5	105		
9		6	76		
10		7	79		
11		8	132		
12		9	102		
13		10	96		
14		11	98		
15		12	100		
16		13	120		
17		14	89		
18		15	117		
19					
20	Standard Deviation:	16.04369			
21					

Variance

As you may have noticed from looking at how standard deviation (s) is computed, the variance (s^2) is merely the standard deviation squared. It is not widely reported in the scientific literature by itself because people cannot intuitively interpret it. It is, however, very useful in later statistical techniques.

Computing the Variance

To compute the Variance, simply square the standard deviation.

Computing Variance in Excel

To compute the variance of a set of scores in Excel, use the **VAR** function.

Figure 17. Variance in Excel.

	A	B	C	D	E
	Clipboard			Font	
		C21		f_x =VAR(C4:C18)	
1					
2					
3		ID	IQ		
4		1	90		
5		2	78		
6		3	98		
7		4	111		
8		5	105		
9		6	76		
10		7	79		
11		8	132		
12		9	102		
13		10	96		
14		11	98		
15		12	100		
16		13	120		
17		14	89		
18		15	117		
19					
20	Standard Deviation:		16.04369		
21	Variance:		257.4		
22					

Key Terms

Standard Deviation, Variance

Section 3.4:
The Normal Curve

N ow that we have an understanding of variance and standard deviation, we can discuss some very useful properties of the **normal curve** that would not have made sense before. First, let us consider some of the properties of the normal curve.

Synonyms of the Normal Distribution

*The normal distribution is also known as the **Bell Curve** since it resembles the outline of a church bell when it is graphed.*

*It is also known by statistically savvy folk as the **Gaussian distribution**.*

It is **symmetrical**. That means that whatever is true of the left side is true of the right side. The distinct bell shape means that a predictable number of subjects will fall within certain specified areas under the curve. We can define these areas in terms of standard deviation units.

Adam J. McKee

The 68% Rule

Recall what standard deviation is: it is the average distance of scores from the mean of a distribution. We can examine the difference score for any particular individual and see how many standard deviations they are from the mean to get an idea of how extreme that score is. One extremely important characteristic of the normal distribution is what we will call the *68% Rule*. The **68% Rule** states that about 68% of cases lie within one standard deviation unit of the mean in a normal distribution.

68% Rule

About 68% of cases lie within one standard deviation unit of the mean in a normal distribution.

Note that when we say "one standard deviation unit" we are talking about both sides of the curve. In other words, we are saying that 68% of people will fall within the interval defined by negative one standard deviation from the mean and positive one standard deviation from the mean. Let us say, for example, that a test has a mean of 100 and a standard deviation of 10. In such a case, 68% of those taking the test would score between 90 and 110. Remember that this rule only applies to a normal distribution! The less normal the curve, then less accurate the rule.

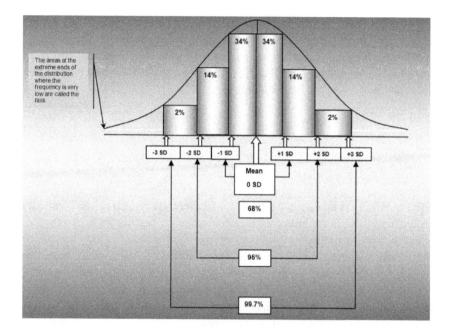

The 95% and 99% Rules

The **95% Rule** says that if you go out two standard deviation units either side of the mean, you will capture 95% of cases. To get the scores that fall two standard deviations from the mean, simply multiply the standard deviation by two and subtract that from the mean to get the lower bound, and add it to the mean to get the upper bound.

For example, let us return to our example test where the mean was equal to 100, and the standard deviation was equal to 10. To find the score that defines the second standard deviation below the mean, we multiply 10 x 2 to get 20. We then subtract 20 from 100 (100 − 20 = 80) to get 80. We then add 20 to 100 (100 + 20 = 120) to get 120. This means that 95% of those taking the test had scores falling between 80 and 120.

95% Rule

About 95% of cases lie within two standard deviation unit of the mean in a normal distribution.

The **99.7% Rule** says that 99.7% (nearly all) of cases fall within three standard deviation units either side of the mean in a normal distribution. To get the scores that fall three standard deviation units from the mean, simply multiply the standard deviation by three and subtract that from the mean to get the lower bound, and add that to the mean to get the upper bound.

99.7% Rule

About 99.7% of cases lie within three standard deviation unit of the mean in a normal distribution.

The 95% Rule is an approximation. To be more precise, you need to go out 1.96 standard deviation units either side of the mean to capture 95% of cases. This seemingly strange number is dictated by the mathematics of the normal curve. Unfortunately, you can have nice round percentages, or you can have nice round standard deviation units, but you cannot have both. The properties of the normal curve just do not allow for it. The approximation is best used for seeing a distribution of scores in your mind's eye. When further statistical analysis is involved, and your results will appear in reports, it is better to use the more precise multiplier.

For example, let us consider an IQ test that has a mean of 100 and a standard deviation of 15. To obtain the score that marks one standard deviation to the left of the mean, we multiply the standard deviation by the constant 1.96 (15 x 1.96) to get 29.4. We then subtract 29.4 from the mean of 100 to get 70.6. To find the upper bound, we add 29.4 to 100 to get 129.4. Thus, we can say that 95% of people will have an IQ score between 70.6 and 129.4.

If we go out 3 standard deviation units either side of the mean, we will capture 99.7% of all cases. Given a choice between a round percentage and a round standard deviation unit, most researchers will choose to have a round percentage of 99.00%. This means that we have to use a multiplier that shaves off that 0.7% leftover. The 99% Rule says that if you go out 2.58 standard deviation units either side of the mean, you will capture precisely 99% of cases.

To review which multiplier to use when working with a particular percentage, consult the table below. These constants are used so frequently in statistics, it is best to commit them to memory.

Percentage of Cases Multipliers	
To Obtain This Percentage of Cases...	Multiply The SD By This...
68%	1.00
95% (approximate)	2.00
95% (precise)	1.96
99%	2.58
99.7%	3.00

Key Terms

Normal Curve, Gaussian Distribution, Bell Curve, Symmetrical

Adam J. McKee

Section 3.5:
Percentiles and
Standard Scores

Up to this point, we have focused on describing a particular variable that contained values for many cases. This section will shift that focus to looking at ways to describe the characteristics of a particular individual in the context of a set of scores.

The data collection process often results in many raw scores. **Raw scores** are scores that have values that depend on how they are measured. Often, this is not a problem because there is a known frame of reference that makes them easy to interpret. A patient monitoring her blood sugar level, for example, has been told by her doctor what the acceptable, healthy range is. Sometimes, there is no frame of reference to help us interpret scores. For example, being told that a child scored 567 on the local school districts Benchmark Exam is meaningless without a framework for interpretation. This information is useless to us because we do not know what a *normal score* is.

Percentiles

Percentiles divide a set of data into 100 equal parts, each consisting of 1 percent of the total. For example, if a student's score on a standardized exam (such as the ACT or GRE) is in the 90th percentile, then the student outscored 90 percent of the other students who took the exam. A **quartile** is a special type of percentile; it divides a data set into four equal parts, each consisting of 25 percent of the total. The first quartile is the 25th percentile of a data set, the second quartile is the 50th percentile, and the third quartile is the 75th percentile. The **interquartile range** identifies the middle 50 percent of the observations in a data set; it equals the difference between the third and the first quartiles.

Standard Scores

One method of helping consumers of research understand the score of a particular individual is to convert the raw score into a standard score. A **standard score**, which is also called a **z-score**, indicates how many standard deviation units a person is from the mean and whether that score is above or below the mean. A z-score of 1.00 means that the person scored exactly 1 standard deviation unit above the mean, a z-score of 2.00 means that the person scored exactly 2 standard deviation units above the mean, and a z-score of 3.00 means that the person scored exactly 3 standard deviation units above the mean.

We know that each of these scores is above the mean because the value of the z-score is *positive*. A *negative* sign indicates that the z-score is that many standard deviation units *below* the mean. Drawing on what we already know about the normal distribution, we can conclude that a z-score of 1.00 puts that person above about 84% of the other subjects. We know this because 50% of all cases will fall *below* the mean, and the area between the mean and the first standard deviation to the right of the mean contains 34% of cases, which we know from the 68% Rule.

We can also infer the practical range of z-scores from the 99.7% Rule. Since almost every case will fall within three standard deviation units of the mean, we can conclude that almost everybody in a given sample will have a z-score of less than 3.0 but not less than -3.0.

Computing an Individual's z-Score

To compute an individual's z-score, use the following formula:

$$z = \frac{X - \overline{X}}{S}$$

Where
X is the persons raw score
$\overline{X}$ is the mean of the raw scores
S is the standard deviation of the raw scores

Note that the numerator in the z-score formula is a difference score. When the difference score is divided by the standard deviation, the result is how many standard deviation units that particular person is away from the mean.

Computing the Percentile Rank in Excel

To compute the percentile rank of a score in Excel, use the **PERCENTRANK** function. Let's say for example that an honor society advisor wants to rank a pool of applicants by GPA.

Figure 19. Percentile Rank in Excel.

		ID	GPA		Percentile
		1	3.87		88.80%
		2	2.97		0.00%
		3	3.23		11.10%
		4	3.36		22.20%
		5	3.44		33.30%
		6	3.49		44.40%
		7	3.55		55.50%
		8	3.62		66.60%
		9	3.67		77.70%
		10	3.93		100.00%

F6 — =PERCENTRANK(D6:D15,D6)

Note that this function does not return an array of values. You must enter a function for each value to get a column of results as in the example above. In the Function Argument dialog box, "Array" is your list of scores, and "X" is the score you want to compute the percentile rank for.

Computing Standard Scores in Excel

To compute a standardized score in Excel, will first need to compute the mean (AVERAGE) and standard deviation (STDEV). Once those values are computed, you can use the **STANDARDIZE** function to compute a standardized score for any score.

Figure 20. Standerdized Scores in Excel.

Clipboard		Font				Ali
F15	▾	f_x	=STANDARDIZE(D15,D17,D18)			
	A	B	C	D	E	F
1						
2						
3						
4						
5			ID	GPA		Standardized
6			1	3.87		1.24
7			2	2.97		-1.89
8			3	3.23		-0.98
9			4	3.36		-0.53
10			5	3.44		-0.25
11			6	3.49		-0.08
12			7	3.55		0.13
13			8	3.62		0.37
14			9	3.67		0.55
15			10	3.93		1.45
16						
17			Average:	3.513		
18			SD:	0.287327		

Note that STANDARDIZE does not return an array. You must set up a function for each score. There are three arguments: "X" is the score you want to standardize, "Mean" is the mean of the distribution, and "Standard_dev" is the standard deviation of the distribution.

Transformed Scores

Because standard scores (z-scores) have a mean of zero and involve negative numbers, they can be confusing to people who have not studied statistics. To get around this problem, researchers often transform standard scores to another scale that does not have negative values. An important example of a transformed standard score is known as a T score. **T scores** are a standardized score with a mean of 50.00 and a standard deviation of 10.00.

To calculate a T score, simply multiply the person's z-score by 10 and then add 50. This can be done for each case to transform an entire set of data. The constant 50 is the mean of the transformed scores. That is, if a person had a z-score of 0.00, they would have a T score of 50.00. Since the standard deviation is 10, you can surmise that the practical range of T scores is 20 to 80 because of the 99.7% rule.

Computing an Individual's T Score

To compute an individual's T score, use the following formula:

$$T = (z)(10) + 50$$

-Where z is the persons standardized score

By following the general method used to compute a T score, we can transform z-scores into a new scale with any mean or standard deviation. For example, we can convert a set of z-scores into IQ scores with a mean of 100 and a standard deviation of 15:

$IQ = (z)(15) + 100$

Key Terms

Raw Score, Standard Score, z-Score, Transformed Score, T Score

Chapter 4: Exploring Relationships

Section 4.1:
Introduction to Effect Size

In the above discussion on standardized scores, we pointed out that comparisons can be made much easier when things are measured on the same scale. The problem of measuring the same thing on different scales is also a problem when we want to examine the differences between groups. Say, for example, that a researcher conducts an experiment using a pretest and a posttest administered after some treatment is given (The d statistic works equally well when an experimental and a control group is used).

She can determine the difference between the pretest score and the posttest score by simple subtraction. The resulting difference is only meaningful in terms of the scale used. We can compute a measure of **effect size** that allows us to consider the magnitude of the difference in terms of standard deviation units.

While there are several variations on measures of effect size, a statistic known as d is one of the most common. The d statistic is sometimes referred to as a **standardized mean difference statistic.** Because it is scaled in standard deviation units, the range of d is usually between -3.0 and +3.0. Note that if d equals zero, then there is no effect. The farther d is from zero, the larger the effect size. The strength is not affected by whether the result is positive or negative—only the magnitude matters.

While many researchers argue against attaching labels to effect sizes, a sort of naming convention has nevertheless developed. It is common to interpret and effect size (d) of 0.5 or greater as a "large" effect, effect sizes between 0.3 and 0.5 as "moderate," and effect sizes between 0.1 and 0.3 as small. Effect sizes less than 0.1 are considered trivial.

The Logic of Effect Size

Many of my students have said that an effect size is a "measure of the effect." This signals that they have missed the logic of computing an effect size. Any time we look at whether something we did experimentally or in practice changes a dependent variable, a couple of questions naturally arise. The first is very basic, and is answered by statistical hypothesis tests: Does this treatment really work? The second question, which is often glossed over in the professional literature, is equally important: Does this treatment work in a meaningful way? In other words, *how well does it work?* To take an example from criminal justice, a small town police executive is interested in reducing a specific type of crime: manufacture of methamphetamine. Let us say that this police policy maker spends $25,000 per year on a new program designed to eliminate clandestine lab operations. At the end of a three-year trial, it is determined that the average number of meth labs is down from 100 to 97. A simple *t*-test tells the investigator that there is a "statistically significant difference" between the means. In practical terms, this means that the methamphetamine reduction strategy most likely works (and the appearance of it working isn't because of sampling error).

Once this is known, another question arises. That question boils down to one of efficacy; the program works, but does it work well enough to keep funding it year over year? Most small towns wouldn't continue to fund a policing initiative that costs $25,000 per year to eliminate a couple of labs when there are many, many labs remaining. The town's folk and civic leaders would want a more *effective* program. That is, one with a larger *effect size*.

Key Terms

Effect Size, Standardized Mean Difference Statistic

Important Symbols

d

Section 4.2: Correlation

O bviously, variables are things that vary. Researchers are often interested in things that vary together, such as when one variable causes another. For example, time spent studying for a statistics test will "cause" an increase in scores on the test. Thus, we expect that time studying and test scores to vary together systematically. Specifically, as the variable "time" increases, the variable "score" also increases. In a relationship such as this, the reverse of the stated relationship is also true.

In our example, as the variable "time" decreases, so too will the variable "score" decrease. It is possible, even common, for one variable to get smaller as another gets larger. Say we are interested in studying the effects of drinking alcohol on driving ability. As the variable "beers consumed" goes up, we would expect the variable "driving ability" to go down.

For some research questions, you need to understand the *relationship* between two variables. For example, if an investor wants to understand the risk (as measured by volatility) of a portfolio of stocks, it is essential to for the investor to grasp how closely the returns on the stocks track each other (move up and down in price together). Researchers can determine the relationship between two variables with two basic **measures of association**: *covariance* and *correlation*. A *measure of association* is a numerical value that reflects the tendency of two variables to move together in the same direction or in opposite directions.

The covariance is a measure of association, but like the variance, it is in a funky metric that we can't intuitively understand. Correlation is a closely related measure. It's defined as a value between −1.00 and +1.00, so interpreting the correlation is easier than interpreting the covariance. If we are plugging the measure of association into another (usually more advanced) statistics, we often use the covariance for mathematical reasons; if we want to interpret the statistic directly, we report the correlation.

When variables are systematically related in either of these ways, then they are said to **covary**. Another word for covariation is **correlation**. The degree of this covariance is often measured with a statistic known as a **correlation coefficient**. A correlation coefficient, then, is a measure of the magnitude of the relationship between two variables.

The most commonly encountered correlation coefficient is **Pearson's *r*** statistic (*r*). Pearson's r ranges in value from -1.0 to 0.0 to +1.0. If the value is zero, then there is no correlation between the two variables. That is, the two variables do not vary together in any systematic way. (This is an oversimplification. In reality, it means that they do not vary together in any *linear* way, but that is a topic for later).

If the value of r is 1.0, then the correlation is said to be perfect. That means that whenever one variable (X) goes up a specified amount, then the other variable (Y) also goes up a specified amount. When this is the case, the value of Y can be predicted with perfect accuracy by knowing X. Thus, a valuable ability of correlation (and later regression) is the ability to predict something by knowing something else.

When both variables increase or decrease together, then the relationship is said to be **positive**. If one goes up and the other goes down in value, then the relationship is said to be **negative**. By convention, if a relationship is negative, a negative sign is placed before the value of r. Thus, a value of -1.0 represents a perfect negative correlation. If there is no negative sign, then we are to assume that the correlation is positive. Note that a correlation coefficient is not a proportion—it cannot be viewed as a fraction of something.

Don't let the signs confuse you; negative signs tell us the direction of the correlation and say nothing about its magnitude or strength.

Scattergram

Correlation coefficients provide us with a single number that summarizes the relationship between two variables. We can also examine this type of relationship visually by creating a scattergram. A **scattergram**, which is also known as a **scatterplot**, shows the relationship between two variables graphically. A scatter plot is designed to show the relationship between two *quantitative* variables.

Usually, the graph is arranged with one variable running up and down the left side (the vertical or *y*-**axis**) and another variable runs along the bottom (the horizontal or **x-axis**). A dot is placed where the two variables intersect for each case. The final pattern we notice in the dots can reveal much information about the relationships between the two variables. If the dots form no discernable pattern and have a circular appearance on the graph, then we can say there is little or no relationship between the two variables.

If the dots form a line, then we have a strong relationship. Perfect relationships will form a perfect line, and moderate relationships will form a shape somewhat like a football. Because these relationships tend to form lines when graphed (or represented mathematically), they are known as *linear relationships*. We can determine the nature of the relationship by examining the slope of the line. If the pattern of dots forms a line from the lower left to the upper right side of the graph, then the relationship between the variables is a *positive* one. If the line runs from upper left to lower right, then the relationship is a *negative* one.

It is often helpful to draw a line through the center of the cluster of dots. This line gives us a clearer indication of the relationship between the two variables when the pattern of the dots is somewhat scattered out. The best such line—the one that fits best—can be determined mathematically. A line so determined is called a *regression line*. We will discuss regression in much more detail in a later section.

Generating a Scatterplot in Excel

To generate a scatterplot in Excel, first, you need to construct a data table that contains scores for your X variable and your Y variable. Once you have the scores entered, highlight both columns of scores. Under the **Insert** tab, find **Charts** and select **Scatter**. In the example below, the first option without any kind of lines was selected. The legend is set up for categorical data, so it was deleted.

Figure 21. Scatterplots Lines In Excel.

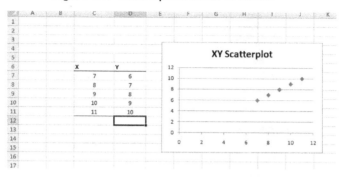

Excel will also fit a regression line to your data points on the chart. To accomplish this, right click over the data points in the chart and select **Add Trendline**. In the dialog box that opens, you can select several line options. At this point, you will want to leave this on the default setting of **linear**. There are also checkboxes at the bottom that allow you to elect to have the equation for the regression line and the quantity R^2 printed above the regression line on your chart.

Figure 22. Regression (Trend) Lines in Excel.

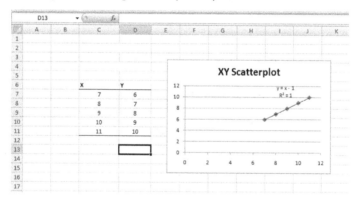

More on Correlation Coefficients

Correlation coefficients are a numerical indicator of the strength of a relationship between two variables. Correlations also tell us the direction of the relationship. By *direction* we mean whether both variables go up or down together (a *positive* or *direct*

95

relationship) or whether one goes up when the other goes down (a *negative* or *inverse* relationship).

The most widely used correlation coefficient is the Pearson r. Note that Pearson's r is a *bivariate* correlation technique. The term bivariate means that *two* variables are represented by the correlation. (We will discuss correlation techniques that consider the relationship between more than two variables in the later section on Multiple Correlations).

The highest possible value of r is 1.00, which represents a perfect correlation. A perfect negative correlation is indicated by a value of -1.00. A value of zero (0.00) indicates that there is no relationship between the two variables. The closer the value of r is to |1.00|, the stronger the relationship. Thus, the magnitude of the value of indicates the strength of the relationship, and the sign shows the direction of the relationship.

To determine the strength (magnitude) of a correlation, we look at the absolute value of the coefficient. For example, a correlation of 0.90 between two variables would indicate a very strong positive relationship, whereas a correlation of 0.20 would indicate a weak (but positive) relationship. A correlation of −0.8 would indicate a very strong *negative* relationship. A correlation of −0.30 would designate a weak negative relationship. A correlation of 0.00 would show that two variables are **independent** (that is, *unrelated*).

Computing Correlation Coefficients in Excel

To compute the correlation coefficient between two variables (Pearson's), use the **CORREL** function. Let's say for example that a researcher is interested in the relationship between students' GPA and hour spent studying.

Figure 23. The CORREL Function in Excel.

	Clipboard			Font			Alignm
	D19	▼	fx	=CORREL(D6:D15,F6:F15)			
	A	B	C	D	E	F	G
1							
2							
3							
4							
5			ID	GPA		Study Hours	
6			1	3.87		10	
7			2	2.97		4	
8			3	3.23		5	
9			4	3.36		6	
10			5	3.44		7	
11			6	3.49		8	
12			7	3.55		9	
13			8	3.62		9	
14			9	3.67		10	
15			10	3.93		12	
16							
17			Average:	3.513		8	
18			SD:	0.287327		2.49	
19			Correlation:	0.97			
20							

Note that the CORREL function yields the same results as the **PEARSON** function.

Coefficient of Determination

The *coefficient of determination* is r squared. It is symbolized much as you would suspect: r^2. It is important to note that a correlation coefficient is not a proportion and cannot be interpreted as such. A correlation of 0.50 cannot be interpreted as half or 50% of anything—correlations simply do not work like that.

The coefficient of determination can be interpreted as a proportion or a fraction. If a correlation is computed to be 0.50, then r^2 will be equal to 0.5 x 0.5 = 0.25. This result of 0.25 is interpreted as the proportion of *variance explained* or the amount of *variance accounted for*. We can easily convert this to a percentage by multiplying r^2 by 100. Thus, with a correlation of r = .50, 25% of the variance in one variable is accounted for by knowing the value of the other variable.

*The **coefficient of determination** tells us what proportion of the variance in one variable that can be accounted for by the variance in another variable.*

Note that we can compute the percentage of variance not accounted for by subtracting the r^2 percentage from 100%. In the above example where $r = .05$, we can determine that 25% of the variance is accounted for, and that 75% of the variance is <u>not</u> accounted for.

It is also important to note that correlation coefficients can be misleading when they are small. This is because the percentage of variance explained shrinks faster than the correlation coefficient seems to indicate.

Pearson's r and Coefficients of Determination			
Pearson's r	Pearson's r^2	% of variance Accounted For	% of variance Not Accounted
1.00	1.00	100%	0%
.90	.81	81%	19%
.80	.64	64%	36%
.70	.49	49%	51%
.60	.36	36%	64%
.50	.25	25%	75%
.40	.16	16%	84%
.30	.09	9%	91%
.20	.04	4%	96%
.10	.01	1%	99%

Computing r-Square with Excel

To compute the coefficient of determination, use the **RSQ** function.

Figure 24. r-Square in Excel.

Clipboard		Font			Alignment

D23 f_x =RSQ(D6:D15,F6:F15)

	A	B	C	D	E	F
1						
2						
3						
4						
5			ID	GPA (Y)		Study Hours (X)
6			1	3.87		10
7			2	2.97		4
8			3	3.23		5
9			4	3.36		6
10			5	3.44		7
11			6	3.49		8
12			7	3.55		9
13			8	3.62		9
14			9	3.67		10
15			10	3.93		12
16						
17			Average:	3.513		8
18			SD:	0.287327		2.49
19						
20			Pearson r:	0.97		
21			Intercept (B):	2.62		
22			Slope (B):	0.11		
23			r-Squared:	0.94		

Key Terms

Covariance, correlation, Correlation Coefficient, Pearson's r, Scattergram, Scatterplot, x-axis, y-axis, linear relationship, positive relationship, negative relationship, Inverse Relationship, Direct Relationship, Regression Line, Trendline, Bivariate, Multiple Correlation, Coefficient of Determination

Important Symbols

$$r, R, r^2, R^2$$

Section 4.3:
Multiple Correlations

A multiple correlation coefficient (R) evaluates the degree of relatedness between a cluster of variables and a single outcome variable. This is a valuable tool for the social science researcher because something as complex as human behavior can rarely be attributed to a single cause. Multiple correlations allow us to examine relationships that are more complex than simple bivariate correlations.

Squaring the multiple correlation coefficient yields the *coefficient of determination*, symbolized R^2. The interpretation of R^2 is identical to r^2, except that R^2 is talking about the set of variables rather than just one.

As a practical matter, the multiple R can be interpreted in the same way as Person's r except that we must keep in mind that R tells us about how a cluster of variables relates to a *criterion variable* rather than a single variable. It is important to know that R is more complex than merely the sum of separate r-values. This is so because the formula subtracts out the variance shared between the predictor variables. This means that the greater the correlation between the predictor variables, the less increase you have in R when they are added. The only time that R is the sum of the individual r-values is when the predictor variables are completely unrelated.

Key Terms

Covariance, correlation, Correlation Coefficient, Pearson's r, Scattergram, Scatterplot, x-axis, y-axis, linear relationship, positive relationship, negative relationship, Inverse Relationship, Direct Relationship, Regression Line, Trendline, Bivariate, Multiple Correlation, Coefficient of Determination

Important Symbols

$$r, R, r^2, R^2$$

Section 4.4:
Linear Regression

When variables are correlated, we can use knowledge of one to predict the value of the other. That is, we can study the relationship between variables that are known, and use our knowledge of that relationship to predict future values when one of the variables is not known. For example, a university admissions office might use your SAT score to predict your success in college based on what they observed about the relationship of SAT scores to college success in past students. The statistical technique that allows us to derive an equation to make such predictions is known as **regression.**

In linear regression, a line is mathematically fitted to the dots on a scattergram. The idea of the line is to split the field of dots down the middle, much like the seam on a football.

By using a mathematical equation derived from the regression line, we can derive a regression equation that allows us to predict the value of an unknown score (y) using information from a known variable (x). A straight line can be represented mathematically by the following formula:

$$\hat{Y} = a + bX$$

Where $\hat{Y}$ stands in for the value we want to predict, **a** is the intercept (the score where the regression line meets the vertical axis) and **b** is the slope of the line (the direction and angle of the line).

Thus to predict a score for **Y** given **X**, we first need to obtain values for **a** and **b**. In the case of multiple regression, this involves some very complex math, and is best accomplished using a computer.

Let us say, for example, a statistics professor is curious as to whether scores on the first test are a valid predictor of scores on a final exam. He enters the scores into a spreadsheet and generates the scatterplot illustrated below. We can determine several things by examining this scatterplot. First, notice the line running through the dots. This is the regression line (also known as a *trend line*). The dots fall "pretty close" to the line, but they do not fall along it exactly. From this, we can tell that the correlation is a strong one, but it is not perfect.

Also, note that R^2 is reported. This tells us that 83.88% of the variance in Y is explained by knowing X.

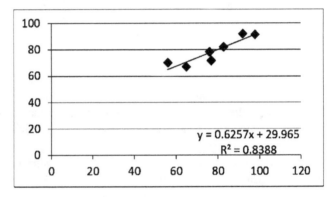

The regression equation is also reported as $Y = 0.6257X + 29.965$. With this equation, we can make future predictions about what Y will be for an individual given X. For example, let us say a student makes a score of 90 on the first exam. What is his final exam grade likely to be? We can easily determine this by multiplying 0.6257 by 90 to get 56.313. The product is then added to the constant of 29.965 to yield a predicted Y value of 86.278.

It is important to realize that linear regression is useful only if the dots form a straight line. If there is no line to speak of or the line must curve one or more times to adequately fit the data, then linear regression should not be used.

Correlation and Causation

It is important to understand that just because we have established a correlation we have not necessarily established a *causal relationship*. In a causal relationship, there is evidence to believe that one variable causes a change in another. While demonstrating a correlation is necessary to claim a causal relationship, it is not sufficient.

Computing the Intercept in Excel

The **INTERCEPT** function computes the point at which the regression line crosses the y-axis, which is known as the intercept.

Figure 25. Intercept in Excel.

Clipboard		Font			Alignme

D21 f_x =INTERCEPT(D6:D15,F6:F15)

	A	B	C	D	E	F
1						
2						
3						
4						
5			ID	GPA (Y)		Study Hours (X)
6			1	3.87		10
7			2	2.97		4
8			3	3.23		5
9			4	3.36		6
10			5	3.44		7
11			6	3.49		8
12			7	3.55		9
13			8	3.62		9
14			9	3.67		10
15			10	3.93		12
16						
17			Average:	3.513		8
18			SD:	0.287327		2.49
19						
20						
21			Intercept (B):	2.62		

Computing the Slope in Excel

The **SLOPE** function computes the slope of the regression line. Note that this function yields non-standardized coefficients.

Figure 26. The slope in Excel.

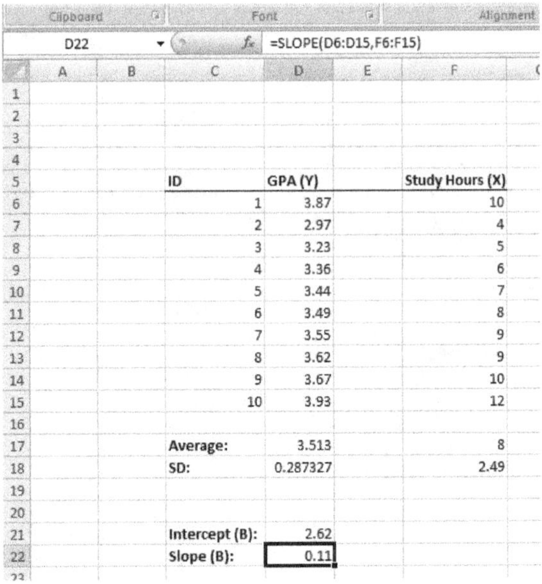

	A	B	C	D	E	F	
				=SLOPE(D6:D15,F6:F15) D22			
5			ID	GPA (Y)		Study Hours (X)	
6			1	3.87		10	
7			2	2.97		4	
8			3	3.23		5	
9			4	3.36		6	
10			5	3.44		7	
11			6	3.49		8	
12			7	3.55		9	
13			8	3.62		9	
14			9	3.67		10	
15			10	3.93		12	
17			Average:	3.513		8	
18			SD:	0.287327		2.49	
21			Intercept (B):	2.62			
22			Slope (B):	0.11			

Predicting Y with Excel

To predict the value of Y given new values of X, use the **TREND** function. The TREND function returns an array containing a predicted Y value for each new value of X.

Figure 27. Predicting Y in Excel

	Clipboard			Font			Alignment			Number
	I6		▼	f_x {=TREND(D6:D15,F6:F15,H6:H8)}						
	A	B	C	D	E	F	G	H	I	
1										
2										
3										
4										
5			ID	GPA (Y)		Study Hours (X)		New X's	Predicted Y	
6			1	3.87		10		1	2.73	
7			2	2.97		4		3	2.96	
8			3	3.23		5		11	3.85	
9			4	3.36		6				
10			5	3.44		7				
11			6	3.49		8				
12			7	3.55		9				
13			8	3.62		9				
14			9	3.67		10				
15			10	3.93		12				
16										
17			Average:	3.513		8				
18			SD:	0.287327		2.49				
19										
20										
21			Intercept (B):	2.62						
22			Slope (B):	0.11						

Note that the **TREND** function returns an array. The results will not be displayed properly of you just select "OK" to close the Function Arguments dialog box. You must press CONTROL + SHIFT + ENTER at the same time to get it right.

Key Terms

Regression, Regression Equation, Regression Line, Slope, Intercept, Causal Relationship

Important Symbols

$\hat{Y}, a, b, X, R, R^2$

Section 4.5: Advanced Regression Models

So far in this text, we've discussed a type of regression that depends on a specific way of estimating the formula for a line. This is sometimes referred to as Ordinary Least Squares (OLS) regression (I'll use the unpretentious name of *regular regression*). Researchers use several different techniques when the assumptions of OLS cannot be met in a particular study. Below we will discuss some of these variants on the "family" of regression techniques. We will consider several of these techniques in more detail in a later section.

Logistic Regression

Regular regression has a basic assumption that the outcome variable is measured on the interval or ratio level. You can "fudge" on this assumption a little when there are lots of categories in a discrete space, such as with GPAs. When the dependent variable is binary (dichotomous) or categorical, then regular regression really doesn't work very well. To solve this problem, some brilliant researchers came up with the idea of **logistic regression**. Logistic regression (aka the logit model) is designed to work with categorical data. The math behind the model is based on probability and can be overwhelming for the non-mathematician.

A rather morbid (pun intended) example of research that used this technique was the development of a scale that predicts the likelihood of trauma victims dying in emergency rooms. Note that death is a binary variable; either the patient died or did not die. There is no such thing as being a little dead. This method works by computing an odds ratio and places particular cases into a category based on the odds.

An annoying characteristic of logistic regression is that since the math is quite different, no R^2 statistic is computed. Several researchers have developed "pseudo R^2" statistics, but none have risen to the top of the heap as an accepted best estimate of shared variance. Probably the most common of these is the "Likelihood Ratio R^2" statistic. There are also no beta coefficients, so researchers tend to talk about "odds ratios" when interpreting individual predictor variables.

Path Analysis

Path analysis is just an extension of multiple linear regression designed to make causal statements about the relationships between a set of variables. A major advantage of path analysis is that it uses **path diagrams** to visually depict the relationships that the researcher proposes. This makes understanding the nature of the researcher's hypothesis must easier in many instances. A path diagram is constructed by first putting down the variable names, and then drawing arrows from the hypothetical causes to the hypothetical effects. The simplest form of a path diagram would be drawing an arrow from a single independent variable to a single dependent variable: $X \rightarrow Y$. Of course, few social scientific theories predict such simple relationships between such small sets of variables. These models can become very complex, and are ultimately limited by the mathematics behind the method.

The regression methodology comes into play when we add **path coefficients** to the path diagram. These take the arrows proposed by the model into account and test them using what is essentially multiple regression analysis. *A path coefficient is a standardized regression coefficient (beta weight).* This type of analysis results in a coefficient that is akin to a simple correlation coefficient and can be interpreted in much the same way. Recall that correlation coefficients can be both positive and negative. The same thing applies to path coefficients, and the interpretation is essentially the same as well. When the researcher hypothesizes that two variables are correlated but is not willing to predict the direction of that relationship, double-headed arrows can be used: $X <--> Y$.

When examining a path diagram, you will sometimes encounter paths that do not have coefficients next to an arrow. This is because researchers often omit path coefficients that do not reach a certain magnitude that they have determined. Researchers often omit path coefficients when the relationship represented by a particular arrow is not statistically significant.

All of this talk of causes and effects in path analysis can be confusing. As we stated in an earlier section, correlations do a poor job of supporting cause and effect statements, especially when compared to true experiments. Those caveats sill apply to path analysis: correlational studies are still correlational studies, no matter how fancy the statistics used to analyze the data are. That is not to say that causal-comparative (correlational) studies have no value, but it does suggest that results be interpreted with extreme caution when evaluating cause and effect statements. Keep in mind that the researcher's decisions as to which way the arrows point is based on theory (hopefully!), and that the converse relationship may, in fact, be the correct specification. Also, there may be some variable not included in the analysis that causes the variables to only appear to be causally related.

A major advantage of path analysis versus other techniques is the ability to clearly model *direct* and *indirect effects*. A **direct effect** is observed when two variables are specified to be causally related. **Indirect effects** are effects that are mediated by an intermediary variable. Let's say, for example, that a researcher is interested in job satisfaction among police officers. She notices that older officers tend to have higher job satisfaction than younger officers. She could specify this relationship as follows: **Age → Job Satisfaction**. She further theorizes that the explanation for this relationship is that veteran officers tend to have higher salaries than "rookies" do, and that this income disparity could explain the differences in job satisfaction. She could model this relationship as follows: **Age → Income → Job Satisfaction**.

The path coefficients are derived by the creation of **structural equations**. Whereas multiple regression analysis typically results in a single equation that describes the relationship between the set of predictor variables and a variable **Y**, structural equations (there are usually more than one) look at specific aspects of a complex set of hypothesized relationships. In other words, structural equations provide coefficients for each arrow in the path diagram.

When creating or interpreting path diagrams, it is useful to distinguish between *exogenous variables* and *endogenous variables*. An **exogenous variable** is "caused" by other variables not considered in the researcher's model. We can quickly identify such variables in a path diagram because no arrows are pointing to them; all of the arrows point away from exogenous variables. With an **endogenous variable**, it is hypothesized that the variance is at least partially explained by one or more other variables in the researcher's model. We can identify such variables because arrows from other variables will point to them. Note that the path to an endogenous variable must be unidirectional in path analysis. That is, you cannot specify causal loops using this analytical method.

When constructing structural equations, it is important to note that predictions made with such equations are seldom perfect. Given the complex nature of human behavior, it is no wonder that a small system of variables cannot perfectly predict an outcome variable. There are other, unconsidered factors in play. These "unknowns" are referred to as "error" in the language of regression analysis. It is important to understand that the term error does not connote a mistake on the part of the researcher; the term is not pejorative when used in this context. It may be helpful to informally define *error* as "stuff not in the model." Many path diagrams will explicitly model the **error term**.

Factor Analysis

If your professor wants to test your "statistical knowledge," it would be unfair to give you a single question and call that your final exam. After all, "statistical knowledge" covers a lot of ground; one question cannot possibly assess it! This is why test authors use several questions to measure a single subject area. The idea of most objective tests, then, is to create a representative sample of all possible test questions over the material at hand. All of those questions can be cumbersome to work with, so researchers like to "boil them down" into simpler variables. Think about your college admission test scores. You had one score for reading, one for math, and another for science. You answered hundreds of questions, but the test folks reduced those down into a small number of variables. These new variables are often called **factors** by researchers. Factor analysis, then, is a method of examining how these many items interrelate. That is a major departure from other methods we have discussed where there was one dependent variable. Factor analysis examines the relationships between many dependent variables. The factors themselves can be seen as the independent variables. Your answer to ten math questions on the SAT may *depend* on your mathematical intelligence (a factor).

Structural Equation Modelling (SEM)

Since the advent of computing technology that allows for the easy integration of graphics into documents, a new convention has developed in how path diagrams are constructed. Latent variable names are set off by putting them in ovals. Observed (manifest) variables are set off in rectangles. In complex models, the "boxes" which represent the variables that the researcher has actually measured are combined in groups as a proxy for the latent variable represented by an oval. Thus, the boxes will have arrows that point to one or more ovals.

This convention is closely related to the more advanced technique that grew out of path analysis: Structural Equation Modeling (SEM). Most researchers today think of path analysis as a special case of SEM. This is because SEM can do the same things that path analysis can do, but it goes farther and has fewer restrictions on how researchers can specify models. Perhaps the most important distinction is that path analysis assumes that all of the measured variables are measured without error, with is rather unlikely. SEMs allow the researcher to specifically model error terms using latent variables. This improves the accuracy of the model.

Recall that **latent variables** are variables that are hypothesized to exist by the researcher (and hopefully the rest of the scientific community), but that cannot be directly measured. Take intelligence for example. Intelligence cannot be directly measured, but few would argue that such a construct does not exist. To measure this construct, psychologists use intelligence test scores to stand in as a sort of proxy for the actual variable of interest. Depression is another common example that comes from psychology. You cannot directly measure depression, but you can measure things that are thought to be symptoms of depression. The relationship of this concept to other statistical techniques becomes clearer when we recognize the fact that latent variables can also be called **factors**. This fact gives us a clue that SEM methods are related in purpose to **factor analysis**.

Model Specification

In this section, I'll cheat a little and go back over some of the hallmarks of good research design in the context of working with SEMs. Never lose sight of the fact that when we specify a structural model, we are in essence specifying a theoretical model. The takeaway from this is that all good models of reality in the social sciences should be derived based on the literature and theory prior to data collection. The purpose of a statistical model, then, is to create a mathematical description of how the world works. If we get the specification right, then the data will "fit" the model to some degree. Also recall that models are oversimplified by definition, and thus the data will never fit the statistical model perfectly. Social scientists are looking for a "good fit" not a perfect one. In fact, in the world of SEMs, researchers often calculate "goodness of fit" statistics to determine the value of their models.

When specifying a structural equation, the researcher will do this (or the software will do it) using variance and covariance matrices. It may be easier to think of covariance in terms of correlations. In other words, the researcher has a theory that specifies a certain set of correlations between a specific set of variables. The way we test the theory is to measure those variables and see if those correlations are indeed there, if they go in the direction the theory predicted, and how strong they are. If the theoretical model doesn't fit the real world data, we reject the model. In SEM terms, the theoretical model was *misspecified.*

Chapter 5:
Hypothesis Testing

In the first chapter, we made passing mention of a family of techniques called inferential statistics. We quickly moved ahead with an in-depth discussion of descriptive statistics, leaving our discussion of statistical inference for some future date. That time has come; this chapter concerns itself with the essence of inferential statistics: testing null hypotheses.

As we move on, we will discuss several different statistical tests. These are all different, and which one you should choose depends on your research question, and by extension the nature of the data that you have collected. While these methods have different assumptions and involve different computations, they all have the same underlying logic. If you understand the logic of hypothesis testing, then you can move on with confidence. If you don't understand why you are doing all these different tests, it becomes a jumbled mess in your mind. Be sure to master the underlying logic of hypothesis testing before you move on to trying to understand particular hypothesis tests!

Section 5.1:
The Logic of
Hypothesis Testing

ecall that all research begins with a research problem. We usually want to
know the answer to a "why" or "how" question. Our proposed solution to
most research problems will specify a relationship between two or more
variables. Our specification of this type of relationship is called our **hypothesis**.

*A **hypothesis** is an explanation of some observable phenomenon.*

Our hypotheses will not be about a **sample**—it will be about a larger **population**
that we cannot measure. Most of the time we are forced to use samples to represent
populations that we want to study. In empirical research, we will measure our
sample on the variables are interested in. From these measurements, we end up
with a bunch of numbers with which we can compute sample statistics. The
problem is that people do not want to know about our sample and our sample
statistics—they want to know about the population from which the sample was
drawn.

Thus, the purpose of inferential statistics is **generalizing** from a sample to a
population. That is, **making inferences** about a population on the basis of a sample.
Recall that the term *population* does not mean the entire population of a country. It
just means everyone in a group that you want to study, for example, all delinquent
juveniles that drop out of school.

A **generalization** is a general statement made by inference from specific cases.

An **inference** is a conclusion that is based on evidence and reasoning.

Such inferences are usually not drawn directly from observed sample statistics. Rather, we usually make statistical inferences by computing **test statistics**. There are many different test statistics that vary depending on the nature of the data. The common thread of all test statistics is to evaluate the probability of an observed characteristic of a sample accurately reflecting the population parameter in which we are interested.

A **test statistic** is a method of reducing a set of data down to a single number that can be used to test a hypothesis.

Causal Modelling

The language we use in the social sciences to talk about research studies is terribly confusing. Often, we talk in terms of relationships. In other words, we talk as though our interests were *associational*. Most social scientists are interested in social problems, and social problems must have causes. That is the ultimate point of the social scientific endeavor: To explain, predict, and ultimately control social phenomena. We don't want to know the *correlates* of crime, we want to know what *causes* crime so we can intervene and keep it from happening. We don't want to know what *correlates* what math anxiety, we want to know what *causes* it so we can intervene, stop it, and help our students do better on tests.

The key to determining causal relationships is assessing *change*. Most conventional statistics do a decent job of describing static things, such as population parameters from a sample. Traditionally, researchers have regarded true experiments as the ultimate tool for making causal statements precisely because true experiments include change in the design—we often refer to this change in terms of a "manipulation of the independent variable by the researcher."

Every student has heard the mantra "correlation does not imply causation." This truism leads us to an important principle: *You cannot substantiate causal claims from associations alone.* At the foundation of every causal conclusion, there must lie some causal assumption that is not testable in observational studies. An **associational concept** is any relationship that can be defined in terms of a joint distribution (think of a covariance matrix) of observed variables. Examples of associational concepts are correlation, regression, likelihood, odds ratio, "controlling for," and so on. Examples of **causal concepts** are randomization, influence, effect, confounding, "holding constant," spurious correlation, intervention, explanation, attribution, and so on. The former can, while the latter cannot be defined in term of the characteristics of observational sample data.

Simply put, social scientists *must* make causal assertions. A few bold researchers make such claims without hesitation, using phrases such as the IV "causes," "predicts," "affects," "influences," "explains," the DV, or simply that "Y depends on X." Many researchers shun such explicit language, choosing instead to couch their underhanded causal claims in *suggestive* language. Phrases such as "Y is associated or related to x" are all too common. This is a sad state of affairs; Researchers must not shy away from making causal claims to the detriment of society. Causal claims are important for society, and it is crucial to understand when researchers can safely make them. This is a critical skillset for researchers and consumers of research alike.

We will follow Pearl's (2009) simple definition of an **effect** "as a general capacity to transmit changes among variables." Note that this definition pointedly left out that the effect can be conveniently described by a linear equation.

Much has been written about the philosophical and logical underpinnings of determining causation. We will not devote any time to these weighty matters. From a more practical perspective, we are concerned more with measuring the effect of a cause. We'll also adopt the classic logic that three conditions must be met before we can make a causal statement about "X causing Y":

1. X must come before Y in time (called **temporal precedence**)

2. X must be reliably correlated with Y (viz., chance must be ruled out)

3. The observed relation between X and Y must not be explained by other causes

The first condition is a matter of common sense and seems logical in our everyday experiences. If I hypothesized that hitting a ball with a bat made it fly out of the ballpark, you wouldn't see anything wrong with my logic. If, however, I theorized that balls flying out of the park made them hit bats, you'd think I was rather illogical. The problem with research situations is that often which came first is not known and cannot be easily determined. Often, researchers turn to theory to bridge this gap. This approach is especially problematic when there are competing theories that postulate opposite causal relationships. In other words, one theory can specify that X causes Y, but another may specify that Y causes X. If temporal precedence can be established, the theoretical conflict can be resolved with conviction.

The second condition also makes a lot of practical sense. As every skeptic asks, "What does that have to do with the price of tea in China?" The very idea behind that colloquial wisdom is that two things that are not related can't possibly have a causal relationship. Note that a correlation is necessary but not sufficient to infer causation. From a mathematical perspective, a correlation between X and Y will be the same in three cases:

1. X causes Y

2. Y causes X

3. Z causes both X and Y

The third condition is the one that poses the most difficulties and has to do with the **exogeneity** of X. That is, X varies randomly and is not correlated with omitted causes. Such apparent correlations caused by some omitted cause is sometimes referred to as a *spurious correlation*.

Suppose that we have conducted an experiment, where individuals were assigned randomly (say using the randomization function in Excel) to an experimental and a control condition which we'll call variable X. The manipulation of the IV came before the outcome (Y) in time, and temporal precedence is thus established. The grouping variable (X) correlates reliably with the outcome. How do we rule out other (Z) causes? There could be an infinite amount of potential explanations as to why the proposed "cause" correlates with the "effect."

One approach to testing the veracity of a causal claim made in this situation is to examine the **counterfactual model**. The counterfactual asks two important questions:

1. If the individuals who received the treatment had in fact not received it, what would we observe on the DV for those individuals?

2. If the individuals who did not receive the treatment had, in fact, received it, what would we have observed on the DV?

And that, in a nutshell, is why researchers make a big deal about random assignment to groups. If random assignment is used, then the individuals in the control and treatment groups are roughly identical at the start of the experiment (that is, before the IV is manipulated by the researcher). At that point (at least in theory) the two groups are interchangeable. In other words, each group is the counterfactual for the other group.

The treatment effect is simply the difference in Y for the treatment and control group. In a randomized experiment, the treatment effect is correctly estimated when using regression analysis (as well as ANOVA models, because ANOVA is just a special case of regression).

An important take away from all this is that the use of an "Experimental Design" doesn't do anything for the veracity of causal statements. You don't get any causal accuracy points for using an ANOVA instead of a regression model. The veracity has everything to do with research design and nearly nothing to do with the statistical analysis.

When the assumptions of randomized assignment do not hold, such as when we are using preexisting groups, there is no way to directly observe the counterfactuals. There may or may not be differences on some important variable; we simply don't know.

Confidence Intervals

There is a huge debate in research circles as to whether tests of statistical significance have any value. Most researchers still think that they do, as evidenced by the massive number of hypothesis tests that still appear in the professional journals. One of the arguments against such tests is that they tend to create a false sense of precision in the mind of the reader, especially if the reader isn't a researcher. When we compute mean, for example, based on sample data, we know that there is some error in the estimate and that it will not perfectly reflect the true mean of the population. When we present a "point estimate" like that, it is misleading. Many researchers advocate reporting confidence intervals to combat the pernicious effects of false precision.

A confidence interval is a *range* of values that is expected to contain the value of a population parameter with a specified level of confidence (such as 90 percent, 95 percent, 99 percent, and so on). We can construct a confidence interval for a population mean by following three basic steps:

1. Estimate the value of the population mean by calculating a sample mean.
2. Calculate the lower limit of the confidence interval by subtracting a margin of error from the sample mean.
3. Calculate the upper limit of the confidence interval by adding the same margin of error to the sample mean.

The margin of error depends on the size of the sample used to construct the confidence interval, whether the population standard deviation is known, and the level of confidence chosen. The resulting interval is known as a confidence interval. A confidence interval is constructed with a specified level of probability.

When we specify a certain percentage for a confidence interval, we are specifying that we expect the true value of the population mean to land within the confidence interval that many times out of 100. Remember, the mean of the *population* is what we really care about, not just a particular sample. The value of the mean for each sample drawn is an *estimate* of the population mean. The sample mean will be slightly different each time a new sample is drawn. If we draw 100 random samples from a population and compute means and confidence intervals for each sample, 95 of the resulting confidence intervals will contain the true population mean. (You can demonstrate this with computer simulations of you have a lot of time on your hands).

Probability in Hypothesis Tests

In the good old days before computers, we evaluated the test statistic by comparing it to a critical value that we looked up in a table in the back of a statistics book. Now computer programs tell us the **probability (p)** associated with the test statistic we computed. *If the test statistic is below our alpha level (e.g., $p < .05$ or $p < .01$) we reject the null hypothesis.* This means that we are really evaluating the probability associated with the test statistic, not the test statistic itself. In fact, knowing that $t = 3.54$ is pretty meaningless to the researcher; the probability associated with at value of 3.54 is critical in making a statistical decision.

*In hypothesis testing, **p** is the probability of rejecting the null hypothesis when it is true for the population, which is sometimes known as a "false positive."*

In general, the purpose of a test statistic is to determine whether the result of the research study is different than you would expect from chance alone. That is, it helps us answer the question "did what we observe in the sample reflect a real relationship, or was it due to sampling error?" (Note that there are many other sources of potential error, but these are research design issues and are beyond the scope of this text).

When we specify how two or more variables are related in the "real world," we have stated a **research hypothesis**. Example: College educated students will earn a higher income than those without a college education.

*A **research hypothesis** is a statement of how two or more variables are related in the population.*

We can specify this in terms of the means of the groups: We would expect the mean of a sample of college-educated people to be larger than the mean income of a group that was not college educated.

We can specify this hypothesis in terms of population means (μ) as follows:

$\mu_1 > \mu_2$

The **null hypothesis** specifies the exact opposite of the research hypothesis—it specifies that no relationship exists in the population. For example, a psychologist evaluating a new anger management therapy would state "the new therapy has no effect on anger levels" as his null hypothesis. If he can reject the null hypothesis (determine that it is very unlikely to be true) then he can accept the alternate hypothesis—the treatment worked.

*A **null hypothesis** is a statement that there is no relationship between the variables of interest.*

The logic of hypothesis testing is that when we draw a sample from a population, we know that the sample will never exactly reflect the value of the population—chance (probability) dictates a difference, however slight. For example, if we flip a coin ten times, we expect that it will come up heads five times and come up tails five times. If we flip the coin ten times, we would not be surprised if it came up heads six times and tails four times. Such a result is not very improbable.

If we flipped the same coin 1000 times and it came up heads 1000 times, we would suspect that something was amiss, such as a trick coin that was heads on both sides. The reason we suspect something besides chance is causing the observed result is that a result of 1000 heads is very, very improbable. The same logic applies to hypothesis testing. If the observed result is very unlikely due to chance, we dismiss chance as a factor and suspect something else is at work. In an experiment, that thing at work is most likely a *treatment effect*.

When we observe a difference in means or a correlation larger than zero in a sample, it can reflect two basic things:

1. The difference we observe in the sample really exists in the population; or

2. The difference we observe is due only to chance, and there really is no difference in the population.

Conventional research standards dictate that the observed difference be much larger than chance alone would cause—this increases our confidence in saying that an observed difference really exists in the population. The focus in hypothesis testing then is determining whether a sample statistic is the result of a real relationship between the variables of interest, or it just looks that way due to a fluke sample. If we can say that the probability of an observation being due to chance is very unlikely such as a less than 5% or a less than 1% chance, we reject chance as a cause of the observed difference. That is, we reject the null hypothesis. In a properly conducted experiment, if chance is not at work, then the only other alternative is that the observed difference is a real difference and would be found in the population if a census could be conducted to observe it.

Researchers will almost never claim to have proven a research hypothesis. This is because of the probabilistic nature of hypothesis testing. There is always a chance that they are wrong in rejecting the null hypothesis. Most of the time, the researcher will say something to the effect that the research hypothesis was *supported*.

p-values

The use of p-values is very often seen in professional journals. It may seem complicated, but the interpretation, at least, is relatively simple. Previously, we discussed the null hypothesis. We said that it is a statement that there is no relationship between your variables of interest—that there is no "effect" in the population (and any observed relationships were caused by chance alone).

The next step is to see if the value you got is very likely if there is, in fact, no relationship in the population. If the value you get is *unlikely* given no real relationship between your variables, then you say that the results are "statistically significant." Another way to express this is that if the result you obtained has a very low probability, then we are willing to say that the null hypothesis is not true (reject it) and that the data support the alternate hypothesis. The symbol p stands for the probability of rejecting the null hypothesis when it is true. Commonly we see a symbolic statement such as "$p < .05$." This tells the reader that the probability of a relationship observed in a sample being caused by chance is less than 5%.

Note that in the traditional language of hypothesis testing, the *lower* the probability, the *higher* the level of statistical significance.

Key Terms

Hypothesis, Sample, Population, Generalization, Inference, Confidence Interval, Test Statistic, Research Hypothesis, Null Hypotheses, p-values, Alpha Level, Type I Error, Type II Error, Power, Assumptions, One-tailed Test, Two-tailed Test

Important Symbols

α, μ, p

Section 5.2: Decision Errors

A fter you have computed a test statistic, a decision must be made. You must either reject or fail to reject the null hypothesis. This part is really easy. You compare the computed probability with your preset alpha level (you did set an alpha level before conducting your test didn't you?) If the probability is less than alpha (less than .05 let us say), you *reject the null hypothesis*. If the computed probability is bigger than alpha, you *fail to reject* the null hypothesis. What makes this process a bit complicated is understanding your chances of being wrong— making what statistics folks call a **decision error**.

Alpha is just a probability threshold that the researcher sets for rejecting the null hypothesis. The alpha level is set by the researcher at the very beginning of the data analysis process—before any test statistics are computed. Some researchers in the social sciences set the value at .05; others set it at the more demanding .01 level. If the probability of your observed relationship is less than the set alpha level (e.g., .01 or .05) then you will reject the null hypothesis.

When it comes to making a decision regarding a null hypothesis, there are only four possible outcomes. If the null hypothesis is true (in the population) and you fail to reject it, you have made a correct decision. If the null hypothesis is false and you reject it, you have made a correct decision. The other two options are incorrect decisions. In other words, you have made a decision error. Researchers have named these *Type I errors* and *Type II errors*.

Alpha (α) *is the probability threshold set by the researcher for rejecting the null hypothesis.*

125

Decision Errors in Hypothesis Testing		
	The Null Is Really True	The Null is Really False
Fail to Reject the Null	Correct Decision	Type II Error (β)
Reject the Null	Type I Error (α)	Correct Decision (1 - β)

A **Type I Error** is also known as a *false positive* because we reject the null hypothesis when it is true. Thus, we have found a "positive" result when we should not have. Alpha (α) is the probability of a Type I Error. When we say that p < .05, we are saying that the chance of making a Type I Error is less than 5%. When we say that p < .01, we are saying that the chance of making a Type I Error is less than 1%.

A **Type I error** occurs when a researcher rejects a null hypothesis when it is true for the population.

A **Type II Error**, also known as a false negative, occurs when the null hypothesis is in reality false (we should reject it) but we fail to do so based on our test results. Beta (β) is the **Type II Error** rate. This is closely related to the **power** of a statistical test, which is defined as 1 − β.

A **Type II error** occurs when a researcher fails to reject the null hypothesis when it should be rejected.

Key Terms

Hypothesis, Sample, Population, Generalization, Inference, Test Statistic, Research Hypothesis, Null Hypotheses, p-values, Alpha Level, Type I Error, Type II Error, Power, Assumptions, One-tailed Test, Two-tailed Test

Important Symbols

α, μ, p

Section 5.3:
Power

M uch of the emphasis in traditional statistical texts is on preventing Type I errors. Little concern seems to be given to the prevention of Type II errors. Type II errors are prevented when a statistical test has sufficient *power*. In hypothesis testing, **power** is the ability of a statistic to detect a significant relationship when one exists. That is, it is the ability of the statistic to correctly reject the null hypothesis.

> **Power** *is the ability of a test statistic to detect a significant relationship between variables when one exists in the population.*

Three factors have an impact on the power of a particular statistic in a particular research situation:

1. The strength of the relationship between the variables (effect size)

2. The predetermined rejection level for the test (the alpha level)

3. The sample size

Power increases as each of these three elements increases. The strength of the relationship is important because stronger relationships are easier to detect than weaker ones. Usually this will be of a fixed magnitude and beyond the control of the researcher. The other two factors are under direct control of the researcher and can be manipulated to increase power.

When it comes to setting an alpha level, the researcher is stuck in a balancing act between committing a Type I error by setting alpha too low, and a Type II error by setting alpha too high. Many researchers have concluded that an alpha of .05 or .01 strikes such a balance. The researcher could set alpha much lower and decrease the risk of a Type I error, but much of the test's power is sacrificed by doing so.

Selecting a sample size is a tricky matter because it is a complex undertaking. For the researcher, samples size is directly related to time and money. Selecting a sample size of 10,000 would certainly result in a powerful test, but would be cost prohibitive in most circumstances. Therefore, the researcher must strike a balance between statistical power and cost-effectiveness. Researchers are advised to conduct a power analysis to determine an adequate sample size (but those methods are beyond the scope of this text). As a consumer of research, you should ask yourself about the researcher's sample size when the researcher reports findings that are not statistically significant.

Section 5.4:
Assumptions

In statistics, the validity of a test statistic depends on several *assumptions* being met. **Assumptions** are things that are taken for granted by a particular statistic. We must verify all of the assumptions associated with a particular statistic when we use it. Some statistics are considered **robust** against violations of certain assumptions. This means that even when the assumption is violated, we can still have a high degree of confidence in the results. As a consumer of research, it is important to understand that if the assumptions of a statistical test are violated, then we cannot trust the statistical outcome or any discussion points the author makes about those results.

> **Assumptions** *are characteristics of the data that must be present for the results of a statistical test to be accurate.*

Common Assumptions

All samples are randomly selected. Most statistical procedures cannot account for systematic bias. Randomly selected samples eliminate such bias and improve the validity of inferences made based on statistical test results.

All samples are drawn from a normally distributed population. Most researchers do not fret over the normality requirement when comparing group means, because the effect of non-normality on *p*-values is very, very small. When a distribution of scores is not normal because of an *outlier*, then the problem can be important to consider. Extreme scores have an extreme impact on the mean, as well as variability and correlation. Recall what we said about the effects of extreme scores on the mean in previous sections. If an extreme score means that you should not use the mean, then a statistical test of mean differences makes no sense either.

All samples are independent of each other. This assumption means that there is no reason that the scores in Group A are correlated with the scores of Group B. If you use the same person for multiple measures of the variable that you are studying, then that person's scores will be correlated. Therefore, if we use a Pretest–Posttest type of design, then we violate the assumption of independent samples. What this means is that we have to use special statistical tests that are designed for correlated scores, often referred to as **repeated measures** tests. Random selection and random assignment to groups are usually considered sufficient to meet this assumption. Statistical tests sometimes are called "independent samples" tests if they have this assumption.

All populations have a common variance. This assumption is often referred to as the **homogeneity of variance** requirement. It only applies to some tests statistics; the most common test statistics that have this assumption are the ANOVA family. Data that meet the requirement have a special name: Homoscedastic (pronounced 'hoe-moe-skee-dast-tic'). Data that violate this assumption (e.g., the two variances are not equal) can be referred to as *heteroscedastic.* If you keep the treatment group and the control group around the same size (equal **Ns**), then this assumption is not really that important. Different variances with widely different sample sizes will taint your results.

Key Terms

Hypothesis, Sample, Population, Generalization, Inference, Test Statistic, Research Hypothesis, Null Hypotheses, p-values, Alpha Level, Type I Error, Type II Error, Power, Assumptions, One-tailed Test, Two-tailed Test

Important Symbols

α, μ, p

Section 5.5: One-tailed vs. Two-tailed Tests

Recall that accepting or rejecting the null hypothesis is based on where a particular test statistic falls within an associated probability distribution. That is, we reject the null hypothesis if the test statistic is sufficiently improbable. We determine this by observing if the probability of such a result falls within the extreme tails of the probability curve. Tails are defined by alpha (α).

It must be considered that if we set alpha at .05 (5%), we are by default saying that we will reject the null hypothesis if the test statistic falls within the most extreme 2.5% found at *both* ends of the distribution. In other words, we are considering two tails of the distribution, not just one. To put this in terms of standard deviation units, we would reject if the test statistic falls past 1.96 standard deviation units to the left or if it falls past 1.96 standard deviation units to the right of the probability distribution. Since we are considering both tails, this type of test is known as a **two-tailed test**.

If we are confident for theoretical reasons that the difference between means is in a particular direction, we can specify a one-tailed test. This moves our 5% rejection region into one tail of the probability distribution. This increases power so long as the mean difference we observe in our sample data is in the hypothesized direction. In our example of a two-tailed test, we reject the null hypothesis if the test statistic is larger than 1.96. For the one tailed-test, we reject the null hypothesis if the tests statistic is larger than 1.65. This lower standard makes it much easier for a researcher to reject a null hypothesis.

Since it is more powerful, it may seem like a good idea to use a one-tailed test all of the time. The problem is that we have to follow some rules that make this less attractive. The most important rule is that if we use a one-tailed test, we must specify that *a priori*. That is, we have to specify the direction of the mean differences before we conduct the analysis. If we later observe that the means were different in the opposite direction than we hypothesized, we must conclude that our findings are not significant.

Key Terms

Hypothesis, Sample, Population, Generalization, Inference, Test Statistic, Research Hypothesis, Null Hypotheses, p-values, Alpha Level, Type I Error, Type II Error, Power, Assumptions, One-tailed Test, Two-tailed Test

Important Symbols

α, μ, p

Chapter 6:
Testing
Null Hypotheses

A troubling aspect of most social science research is that most such research is based on samples. Recall from our earlier discussion of sampling that there are good ways to draw samples from a population, and there are some really, really bad ones. The good ones tend to be based on randomization. The problem with random samples is that sometimes (although rarely) they do not reflect the population that they are drawn from. For example, it is *improbable* that a random sample of 100 students from a particular state university would contain only males. Note my use of the word improbable, and the conspicuous fact that I didn't choose *impossible*.

The word *impossible* cannot be used because improbable things do happen sometimes. People are struck by lightning. People win the lottery. People find buried treasure while digging in a field. Regardless whether the improbable thing is seen as good or bad, such things sometimes happen. Some of these things are completely unpredictable because we simply do not know enough about the phenomenon to say what the probability is. Scientists dislike such things. Things like the lottery make social scientists a lot more comfortable, simply because there is enough information to compute a precise probability of winning (although most scientists would look at the probability and save their money). It is bad enough that you cannot be sure about something, but it is a small comfort to know just how unsure you are.

When it comes to using samples to conduct research, the researcher can never be 100% sure that a particular "treatment" worked as hypothesized. There is always the nagging possibility that the sample was biased (just by random chance) toward making it seem that the treatment worked when it really didn't.

Let's go back to a very early section of this text and recall how a simple experiment works. Let's say, for example, that a pharmacology researcher has developed a new drug that will lower blood pressure. To find out whether the drug works or not, she will conduct an experiment. The simplest way to do this would be to randomly assign people to an experimental group (those that get the new drug) and a control group (those that get a placebo). After administering the drug and the placebo to the appropriate participants in the study, the pharmacologist records the blood pressure of everyone on both groups.

The data are entered into a spreadsheet, and a mean is calculated for both groups. If the control group has a lower mean blood pressure than the experimental group, then it is likely that the drug does not work. If the mean of the treatment group is lower than the mean of the control group, it is evidence that the drug worked as hypothesized. *However,* there is a second alternative that sticks in the mind of the researcher like a splinter: What if the participants in the experimental group had a lower blood pressure than the participants in the control group just because of the way the groups were randomly assigned?

Most of the time randomization will take care of this problem, but not all of the time. There is a small chance that the randomization process created a group with a low or a high blood pressure—purely by chance. The bottom line is that *when you conduct well-designed research using samples, it is possible (but improbable) that you will be wrong in concluding that the treatment worked.*

Social scientists cannot abide qualitative descriptions such as a "small chance." To be satisfied, an exact probability must be established. That is, the social scientist is much more content with the results of the experiment if it can be said that "there is a 5% chance that I am wrong" or that "there is a 1% chance that I am wrong." The social scientific research process requires that the researcher "draw a line in the sand" on this point.

That is, the researcher must specify how much of a chance of being wrong is acceptable when saying that "the treatment worked." The choice of 5% and 1% above was no accident: These are two commonly accepted thresholds among the scientific community. Before we delve deeper into the idea of hypothesis testing, we must first understand a little more about how we know what the chances of being wrong are.

Section 6.1: Error and Confidence Intervals

In social scientific research utilizing samples, population parameters are often estimated using sample statistics. For example, the mean of a sample is often used to approximate the mean of the population. When we do this, we go into the process knowing that our sample mean will be different from the population mean (this idea applies to *any* statistic that we can compute based on sample data; we're just focusing on a single statistic—the mean— right now to keep things from getting confusing). The process is useful because most of the time, the sample mean will be very close to the population mean. There are times, however, that we'll be way off the mark. The rules of mathematics and probability allow the researcher to estimate how big the discrepancy (difference) between the sample mean and the population mean is likely to be. One such estimation is known as the **standard error** of the mean.

To understand how standard error works, it is important to understand what a *sampling distribution* is. Suppose that we have a standardized test with a population mean of 100.00 and a population standard deviation of 15.00. As with most research situations, *we have no idea what these population values are in reality.* We will need to estimate them using sample data. As we previously discussed, there will always be some discrepancy between any given population parameter and its corresponding sample statistic. Say for example that we took a sample from our standardized test with a mean of 100.00. It is very unlikely that we would get a sample with a mean of exactly 100.00. Most samples, however, would result in a mean very near the actual mean, with extreme deviations being very rare.

If we obtain all possible samples of a particular sample size (n) from a given population, and then compute a statistic (mean, standard deviation, proportion, etc.) for each sample, the probability distribution of that statistic is called a **sampling distribution**. This idea is extremely useful when we examine it in light of the *central* *limit theorem.* The **central limit theorem** states that the sampling distribution of any statistic will be approximately normal if the sample size is large enough. (As a rough rule of thumb, many researchers say that a sample size of 30 is large enough). Remember that the means only vary from each other because of random chance due to random sampling error. *These rules do not apply to systematically biased samples.*

In our hypothetical example, the mean of the sampling distribution would be 100.00, and other sample mean values would cluster around the population mean in a normal distribution. The standard deviation of a sampling distribution of means is known as the **standard error of the mean**. Of course, we do not actually know the standard deviation of the sampling distribution, so we use the standard deviation of the sample as an estimate of it.

The **standard error of the mean** (SE_M) is an estimate of the amount of error in estimating the mean of a population based on sample data. Recall that there will always be chance error (i.e., sampling error) that crops up in samples drawn from populations by random selection. The standard error of the means tells us how large that error is *likely* to be.

When we report the value of an estimate for a population, it is often called a **point estimate**. It is so called because it represents a single point estimated to be the mean of the population based on the sample data. Some critics argue that reporting point estimates can be misleading. After all, we know that it is unlikely that the population mean is exactly equal to the one we estimated using the sample data. It would be better, they argue, to provide a range within which we can be fairly sure the population mean really falls.

The standard error of the mean allows us to construct a *confidence interval.* A *confidence interval* is simply a range within which we are fairly sure (to a degree specified by the researcher) the population mean will fall. When we report such an interval, we are said to be reporting an **interval estimate** rather than a single point estimate. When a researcher reports a 95% confidence interval (CI) for a mean, we can have 95% confidence that the true mean lies within that interval. The **true mean** is the mean of the population if we could somehow determine it (which we can't, or we wouldn't be doing sample research in the first place). Obviously, if we had a complete set of data for the population, we would not be using samples. Therefore, we have to estimate how good an estimate the sample mean is of the population mean.

Computing the Standard Error of the Mean

Standard Error of the Mean (SE_M) is a simple computation involving the standard deviation of the scores and the sample size. The formula is as follows:

$$SE_M = \frac{SD}{\sqrt{N}}$$

Confidence intervals for estimated means are very easy to construct once you have computed the standard error of the mean. Recall the earlier section where we examined areas under the normal curve in terms of standard deviation units. The 68% Rule, the 95% Rule, and the 99% Rule apply to sampling distributions just as they did with frequency distributions.

Computing Confidence Intervals for the Mean

Use the following formulas to compute the lower limit and upper limit for the 68%, 95%, and 99% Confidence Intervals:

- $CI_{68} = \overline{X} \pm (SE_M)$
- $CI_{95} = \overline{X} \pm (1.96)(SE_M)$
- $CI_{99} = \overline{X} \pm (2.58)(SE_M)$

Recall that the constants 1.96 and 2.58 are the same ones we learned about previously.

You may have wondered why researchers do not simply compute a 100% confidence interval so that they are sure the mean falls within in it. The problem with that goes back to the very nature of sample research: It is probabilistic. Random sampling produces some degree of error. Unfortunately, we can only estimate the magnitude of that error. The only way to be 100% confident that the mean lies within the confidence interval would be to construct a confidence interval within which all possible means fall. This would merely tell us the minimum and maximum possible score and would be essentially useless.

Adam J. McKee

Key Terms

Standard Error of the Mean, Point Estimate, Confidence Interval, Interval Estimate, True Mean

Section 6.2:
t-Tests

n experimental research, the researcher will often have an experimental group and a control group. The t-test is designed to allow the researcher to test hypotheses about the differences between the means of these two groups. Ultimately, as with most other statistical significance tests, t-tests yield a value of p, which indicates the probability that random sampling errors caused the observed difference between the means and not the treatment.

If the value of p is less than the established alpha level, then the researcher rejects the null hypothesis. The lower the probability, the more confidence the researcher can have in rejecting the null. For a t-test, the null hypothesis simply states that there is no difference between the two means.

A common method of presenting the results of several t-tests is to present all the results together in a table. These tables will usually contain the frequency, the mean, the standard deviation, and the value of t. The probability of t is usually provided in the form of footnotes. Often, one asterisk will denote that the mean differences are significant at the .05 level, and two asterisks signify the differences are significant at the .01 level. This convention, however, is by no means universal. Inspect the footnote carefully to determine the level of significance each time you encounter such a table. A value for t presented without a footnote suggests that the difference between the means was not statistically significant.

t-Test for Independent Groups

Suppose we are interested in a new method of teaching statistics to undergraduate students. To test this new method, we take 100 student volunteers and randomly assign them to two groups of 50. For the control group, we teach statistics as usual. For the experimental group, we use the new method. At the end of the experiment, we give them a test to determine their level of knowledge of the material. Because they are randomly assigned, there should be no relationship between the members of the first and second group. Because there is no correlation between the experimental and control group, then they are said to be **independent groups**.

t-Test for Independent Groups

-The Independent-groups t-test compares the means for two groups of cases.

-Ideally, subjects should be randomly assigned to two groups, so that any difference in scores is due to the treatment and not to other factors.

-The observations should be independent, random samples from normal distributions.

Computing the t-Test for Independent Groups

To compute the value of t, use the following formula:

$$t = \frac{\overline{X}_1 - \overline{X}_2}{S_{DM}}$$

Where:

$\overline{X}_1$ is the mean of the group with the highest mean

$\overline{X}_2$ is the mean of the group with the lower mean

S_{DM} is the standard error of the difference between the mean

To compute the value of S_{DM}, use the following formula:

$$\sqrt{\left[\frac{(N_1 - 1)(s_1^2) + (N_2 - 1)(s_2^2)}{N_1 + N_2 - 2} \right] \left[\frac{1}{N_1} + \frac{1}{N_2} \right]}$$

Where:

N_1 is the number of cases in group 1

N_2 is the number of cases in group 2

s_1 is the standard deviation of group 1

s_2 is the standard deviation for group 2

To ensure the correct solution, remember to follow the order of operations rules.

t-Test for Independent Groups in Excel

Given a computed value of *t*, you can look up the critical value of *t* in a table, or you can get a computer to compute a probability. Just as the computer can compute a value of *p* given *t*, it can compute a value of *t* given *p*. To those of us used to calculating t and then looking up a critical value to compare it with to determine its probability, this inverse way of doing things seems counterintuitive. Strange though it may seem, this is how you must approach the computation of a t-statistic in Excel.

The first step is to place your data into columns. In the language of traditional experimental research, X_1 is the experiential group scores, and X_2 is the control group scores. The next step is to compute the probability associated with the *t* statistic using the **TTEST** function. Examine the dialog box for this function below:

Figure 28.   The t-Test Function Argument Dialog Box.

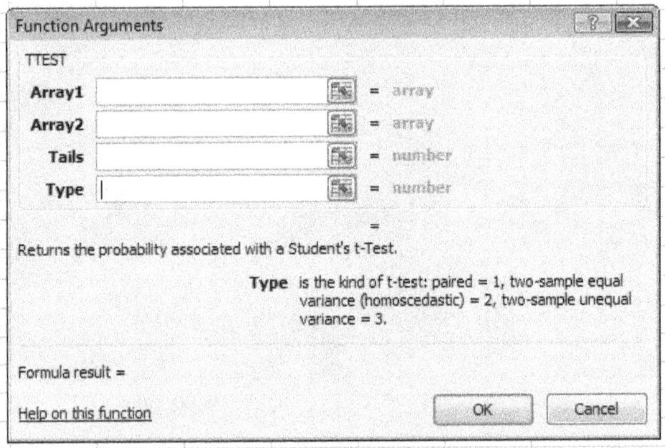

Note the help text for "Type" at the bottom of the box. To choose which type of *t*-test you want the probability reported for, select the appropriate number. That is, the way you do all t-tests is the same in excel. You determine the type of test (dependent or independent samples) by the options you choose in the Function Arguments box. Since we are working with independent data, we enter 2 for "two-sample" which is synonymous with "independent." For tails, enter 2 to let Excel know that we are conducting a two-tailed test. Array1 is the block of cells that contain the values for X_1, and Array2 is the block of cells that contain the values for X_2.

Note the results in the Figure below. The value of *t* is computed using the **TINV** function, which produces the inverse value of a probability of *t*. This is a fancy way of saying that given the probability of *t*, it gives you *t*. Note the number cell **H8** in the function box as the last argument for the **TINV** function. It represents the degrees of freedom, $N - 2$.

Figure 29.   t-Test for Independent Groups in Excel.

B	C	D	E	F	G	H
					f_x =TINV(H10,H8)	
		Experimental	Control		Mean Difference =	1.800
	ID	Grop	Group		N =	20.000
	1	8	7		df =	18.000
	2	9	7		t =	2.475
	3	7	4		p =	0.023492
	4	8	6			
	5	6	4			
	6	7	5			
	7	5	3			
	8	4	3			
	9	7	6			
	10	9	7			
SUM		70.00	52.00			
Mean		7.00	5.20			
SD		1.63	1.62			

Note that the mean difference was computed by simply placing a subtraction problem in the function box for the cell (70.00 – 52.00). For the Independent t-test, the degrees of freedom is equal to the number of subjects in *both groups* minus two (N -2).

Excel Tip: The COUNT Function

When you have a large set of data and do not want to take the time to count the value of N, Excel can do it for you using the COUNT function. Simply insert the COUNT function into an empty cell, and highlight the range of cells that you wish to count. If you have data that you want to be counted in multiple columns, then enter them into different "value" boxes in the Function Argument box.

t-Test for Dependent Groups

When participants in a study are measured, given a treatment, and then measured again (called a repeated measures design), the score on the second measures will be very similar to the first because the measurements come from the same person. Experimental groups that are established this way are said to be **dependent groups**. Dependent groups can also be formed by **matching** subjects on variables the researcher thinks are important to the outcome of a study. When a researcher is interested in testing the difference between the means of two dependent groups, then the **t-test for Dependent Groups** is appropriate. This test is also known as the *t*-test for *correlated data* and the *t*-test for *paired data*. The difference between the *t*-test for dependent groups and the *t*-test for dependent groups is a matter of how *t* is computed. There is no difference in how *t* is reported and interpreted.

t-Test for Dependent Groups

-The t-test for dependent groups compares the means of two variables for a single group (or two functionally equivalent groups as with matching).
-The test computes the differences between scores on the two variables (e.g., pretest and posttest scores) for each case and tests whether the average differs from zero.

t-Tests with Effect Size

Finding that a difference in a sample likely represents a difference in the population fails to answer one important question: How big is the difference? All rejecting the null hypothesis tells us is that there is very likely a difference between the means in the population. To understand the size of the difference, we must look at the actual means. A potential problem with examining the mean differences is the matter of scale. If one researcher is using a 100-point scale to measure intelligence, and another is using a 200-point scale, then the means are not comparable, nor are the mean differences. We are comparing apples and oranges.

One way to get around this problem is to standardize the differences by computing a measure of **effect size**. The most commonly reported measure of effect size for t-tests is a statistic known as Cohen's d. While various researchers utilize different variants on the formula, the most basic method of computing d is to divide the difference between the two means by the standard deviation of the pretest scores. This in effect standardizes the difference between the means in standard deviation units. Recall that the practical limit of standard deviations is +3.00 and -3.00. The takeaway from all this is simple: d is simply a measure of the difference between two means, measured in standard deviation units.

While the matter is hotly debated among researchers, a sort of convention for describing various effect sizes has developed. An effect size of less than .1 is considered "trivial." An effect size between 0.1 and 0.3 is considered "small," and effect size between 0.3 to 0.5 is considered "moderate" and an effect size greater than 0.5 is considered "large." When d is close to zero, there is no effect. Note that as with correlations, the sign of d does not indicate magnitude; it indicates direction. Thus, an effect size of -0.5 is of equal magnitude (largeness) as an effect size of +0.5.

Another commonly reported measure of effect size is r. This r is interpreted in the same way that Pearson's r is interpreted. It is a correlation, and r^2 can be interpreted as the proportion of variance that the two variables share. As we will demonstrate below, you can compute this term given data that violate the assumptions of Pearson's r if you have already done a t-test.

It is important to understand that effect size and statistical significance are largely unrelated concepts. When a social scientist conducts an experiment, is hypothesized that the treatment will have an *effect*. Statistical significance just says that there is a specified percent chance (100% - Alpha) that the effect exists. That is, the observed differences between the means of the groups are very unlikely to be caused by random chance in the assignment process. The logic of hypothesis testing dictates that if chance is not to blame, then it must be the treatment causing the observed differences. This gives the researcher strong support that the treatment worked. Statistical significance is silent on the issue of how well or to what degree the treatment worked (although more "powerful" effects lend power to null hypothesis significance tests). In contrast, that is exactly what a measure of effect size like Cohen's *d* does. It tells us how big the effect is. It does this in terms of the sample standard deviations.

What all this suggests is a two-part question that the researcher must ask: First, does the effect exist? We answer this question with a statistical significance test. If we reject the null hypothesis and accept the idea that the effect exists, then we must ask a second question: How big (magnitude) is the effect? We answer this by computing a measure of effect size.

Computing d and r In Excel

The actual formulas original proposed for *d* are quite different than the ones below. These are what many call *computational formulas*—the logic of why they work is not readily apparent. They have the advantage of being easy to compute and easy to enter into a spreadsheet, which is why we will use them rather than the more informative *heuristic formulas*.

$r = \text{sqrt}((t^2) / ((t^2) + (df * 1)))$

$d = (t*2) / (\text{sqrt}(df))$

Where:

r = Effect Size

d = Cohen's *d* Value (Standardized Mean Difference)

t = t-Test Value

| *df* | = | Degrees | of | Freedom. |

In Excel, **SQRT** is the square root function. For t-squared, just substitute the cell that you are using to enter *t* multiplied by itself. The *df* in the formula must be swapped out for the cell containing the *df* value. Here is an example of how this might look in Excel:

Figure 30. Computing Cohen's *d* in Excel.

	A	B	C	D	E	F	G	H	I
B7			f_x =(B3*2)/(SQRT(B4))						
1	Effect Sizes for t-Tests in Excel								
2									
3	Computed t:	3.2200		The value of t you computed in a t-test goes in this cell.					
4	df:	28.0000		The degrees of freedom for the t-test goes in this cell.					
5	r =	0.5198		The value of r is computed in this cell.					
6	r²=	0.2702		The value of r-squared is computed in this cell.					
7	Cohen's d =	1.2170		The value of Cohen's d is computed in this cell.					
8									
9	Formula for r	=SQRT((B3*B3) / ((B3*B3) + (B4 * 1)))							
10	Formula for r²	=B5*B5							
11	Formula for d	=(B3*2)/(SQRT(B4))							
12									
13	Adam McKee								
14									

Computing the t-Test for Dependent Groups

To compute the value of t, use the following formula:

$$t = \frac{\overline{X}_1 - \overline{X}_2}{S_{MD}}$$

Where:

$\overline{X}_1$ is the mean of the group with the highest mean

$\overline{X}_2$ is the mean of the group with the lower mean

S_{DM} is the standard error of the mean difference

To compute the value of S_{MD}, use the following formula:

$$S_{MD} = \sqrt{\frac{\sum D^2 - (\sum D^2) \div N}{N(N-1)}}$$

Where:

- D is the difference between *pairs* of means
- N is the number of *pairs* of cases

147

The degrees of freedom are:

N-1

Where:

- N is the number of *pairs* of scores

To utilize these formulas, take the following steps:

- List the two sets of scores (X_1 and X_2), making sure that each pair stays matched.
- Create a third column that contains the difference score D $(\overline{X}_1 - \overline{X}_2)$
- Create a fourth column for the square of D (D^2)
- Sum each column
- Plug the information from the column sums into the S_{MD} formula and solve it

Plug the computed value of S_{MD} into the formula for t and solve it

Computing a Dependent Sample t-Test in Excel

To the student experienced with computing t-tests by hand, the method that is used in Excel seems somewhat backward. The trick is to compute the probability, then you get the inverse of the probability to determine the value of t.

The first step is to place your data into columns, taking care to keep X_1 and X_2 paired. The next step is to compute the probability associated with the t statistic using the **TTEST** function. Examine the dialog box for this function below:

Figure 31

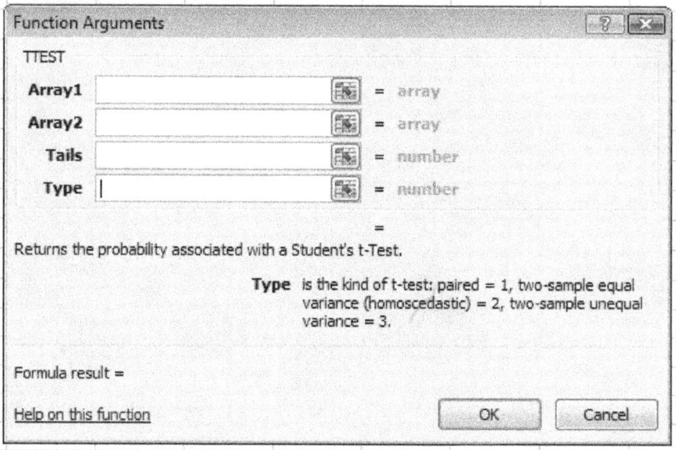

Note the help text for "Type" at the bottom of the box. To choose which type of t-test you want the probability reported for, select the appropriate number. Since we are working with dependent data, we enter 1 for "paired." For tails, enter 2 to let Excel know that we are conducting a two-tailed test. Array1 is the block of cells that contain the values for X_1, and Array2 is the block of cells that contain the values for X_2.

Note the results in Figure 32 below. The value of t is computed using the **TINV** function, which produces the inverse value of a probability of t. This is a fancy way of saying that given the probability of t, it gives you t. Note the number 6 in the function box as the last argument for the **TINV** function. It represents the degrees of freedom, $N-1$.

Figure 32.   Results of a Dependent t-Test in Excel.

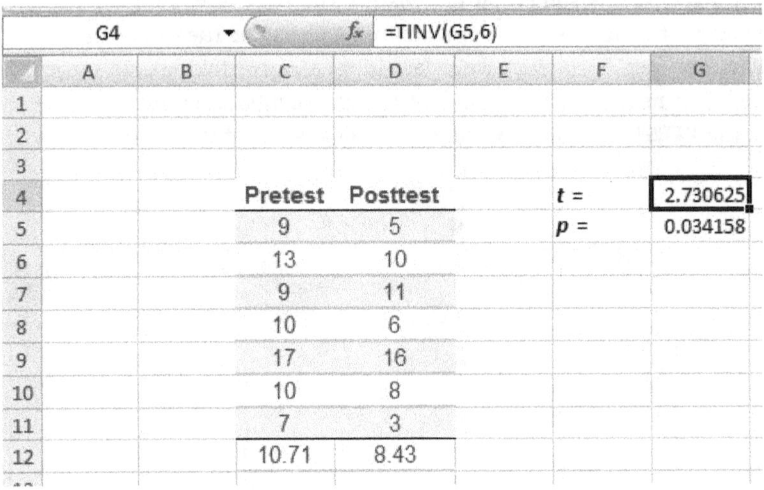

G4			f_x =TINV(G5,6)				
	A	B	C	D	E	F	G
1							
2							
3							
4			**Pretest**	**Posttest**		**t =**	2.730625
5			9	5		**p =**	0.034158
6			13	10			
7			9	11			
8			10	6			
9			17	16			
10			10	8			
11			7	3			
12			10.71	8.43			

Key Terms

t-Test, Independent Group, t-Test for Independent Groups, Dependent Groups, Matching, Correlated Data, Paired Data

Section 6.3:
Non-parametric Tests

Recall that most of the statistical tests that we have discussed so far have several assumptions. Most common among these are the assumption that the data are normally distributed, the assumption of homogeneity of variance, and the assumption that the data are measured at least on the interval level. Because a normal distribution of the data is not an assumption, non-parametric tests are often referred to as *distribution-free tests*.

Parametric tests are so called because they make assumptions about population parameters; non-parametric tests are best used when those assumptions are violated.

Non-parametric tests are encountered in the social science literature much less frequently than their parametric counterparts. This is because the parametric statistics that we previously discussed are more powerful. That is, everything else being equal, they are more likely to allow the researcher to reject a false null hypothesis. Thus, non-parametric tests are usually only used when the assumptions of the appropriate parametric tests are violated to such a degree that the results would be erroneous or misleading.

Chi-square

Whereas the *t* and *F* tests we have previously discussed examine the differences between means, chi-square is a test of the difference between *frequencies*. This test is also identified by its Greek letter designation, χ^2. The null hypothesis for the chi-square test asserts that the observed differences in frequencies were a result of sampling error. Like the other significance tests we have discussed, the null hypothesis is rejected when the probability of the null hypothesis being true is low, such as $p < .05$ or $p < .01$. It is important to note that when the frequencies are statistically different, then the percentages based on those frequencies are also statistically different.

The way the chi-square test works is relatively simple. Rather than comparing means, we compare *observed frequencies* with *expected frequencies*. **Observed frequencies** are the result of our experimental observations. **Expected frequencies** are the values that we would expect of the null hypothesis was true. These are usually expressed as **O** and **E** in the formulas. Often, the expected frequencies are the total sample split into even groups. For example, if we have a variable with four possible conditions, we could assume that if there were no differences in frequencies, then 25% of the subjects would fall into each group. Anything that differs from 25% suggests that the null hypothesis may be false.

This strategy does not make sense all the time, such as when theory suggests that the groups should be of different sizes. Let us say we are interested in the variable gender in a retirement community residents. It would be imprecise to set the expected frequencies at 50% male and 50% female because we know that among the elderly, women are represented in higher numbers because they have a longer life expectancy than men do.

Like the ANOVA designed we discussed in earlier chapters, chi-square tests can be thought of as having *ways* (synonymous with *factors* in parametric tests). When one variable with several levels is being compared (such as political party with the possible values of Democrat, Republican, and Independent), the test can be considered a *one-way* test.

Note that when we refer to the *variable* being analyzed with a chi-square test, we are usually referring to a grouping variables measured at the nominal level. What we are generally measuring is how many individuals fall into a particular group. Unlike with mean difference tests, you will never see a table of means and standard deviations reported with a chi-square test because these statistics are inappropriate given the measurement level of the data.

With the two-way chi-square, we are looking are defining group membership using two categories. When we put this into a table, it is often referred to as a *contingency table*. A contingency table is a statistical table that classifies subjects according to two nominal (grouping) variables with columns representing one variable and rows representing another variable. To confuse matters further, contingency tables are also called **cross-tabulations** or **crosstabs**. Discussions about chi-square results often refer to cells and cell values. This is because there is a cell and a frequency for that cell for each possible combination of variables.

Let us say for example a researcher is interested in the relationship between support for the death penalty and gender. Here we have two variables, each with two levels. We can arrange those into a simple table:

Computing the One-Way Chi-Square

To solve for chi-square, use the following formula:

$$\chi^2 = \sum \frac{(O-E)^2}{E}$$

Where:

- is the observed frequency
- E is the expected frequency

Note that the quantity $\frac{(O-E)^2}{E}$ must be computed for each level of the variable, and then those results are summed.

For the one-way chi-square, the *degrees of freedom* is equal to the number of groups minus 1.

Figure 33.   Cross Tabulation Table.

	Death Penalty Support	
	Yes	No
Male		
Female		

The table above represents the simplest form of two-way chi-square. Since each variable (support for the death penalty and gender) has two levels, this can be referred to as a 2 x 2 contingency table.

In a research situation where there is not a reason to assume that cell frequencies will be equally divided, we can compute an expected frequency based on the assumption that the frequency for one variable should be evenly split across the other variable. In our death penalty example, we have no idea how many people we should expect to support the death penalty. However, if there were no relationship between death penalty support and gender, we would expect both genders to have the same frequency.

Computing the Two-Way Chi-Square

To solve for chi-square, use the following formula:

$$\chi^2 = \sum \frac{(O-E)^2}{E}$$

Where:

- O is the observed frequency
- E is the expected frequency

Note that to use the two-way chi-square, you must first construct a contingency table that creates a cell for all possible combinations of both variables under consideration.

You must then compute the quantity $\frac{(O-E)^2}{E}$ for each cell in the contingency table.

The degrees of freedom for the two-way chi-square is computed as follows: (number of rows − 1)(number of columns − 1)

Note that the magnitude of chi-square is directly related to how big the difference between the observed frequency and the expected frequency is. The larger the value of chi-square, the more likely we are to have statistically significant results. This stands to reason since the bigger the difference between the categories, the more comfortable we are saying that there are real differences and we did not get those results by sampling error. From this, we can see that a large difference between the observed and expected frequencies increases the power of a particular test, just as a large difference between means increases the power of *t* and *F* tests.

The accuracy of chi-square depends on how well the probability of the calculated value of chi-square is described by the chi-square distribution. In other words, the sampling distribution does not fit the table values we use to reject the null hypothesis. The smaller the sample size, the worse the fit. While there is some disagreement among statisticians, a common rule of thumb is not to use chi-square if one or more of the *expected* frequencies falls below five. We can flip this to say that it is a basic assumption of the chi-square test that the expected frequency of all cells has a value above five.

Computing Chi-square Probability with Excel

To compute the probability associated with a chi-square text, use the **CHIDIST** function. Given the value of chi-square and degrees of freedom, CHIDIST returns the probability.

Figure 34. Chi-square Probability in Excel.

Clipboard			Font		Alignment
F14	▾		f_x	=CHIDIST(F11,F12)	
	A	B	C	D	E	F
1						
2						
3						
4						
5						
6						
7						
8						
9						
10						
11					Chi-Square:	3.34
12					Degrees of Freedom:	2
13						
14					Probability:	0.19
15						

Note that you would expect **CHITEST** to yield the value of chi-square. It does not. It returns the value of the probability associated with the chi-square and is identical to **CHIDIST**.

Key Terms

Chi-square, cross tabulation, observed frequency, expected frequency, nonparametric tests

Section 6.4:
Significance and Correlations

As with the mean difference tests (e.g., t and F), a researcher can examine the probability associated with a particular correlation and determine if that correlation is statistically significant. The null hypothesis, however, is different with correlation coefficients. The null hypothesis for a correlation is essentially that there is no real correlation in the population. If true, this means that any observed correlation was due to chance—sampling error. Rejecting or failing to reject the null is associated with a probability, just as with other hypothesis tests. That is, most researchers reject the null hypothesis when $p < .05$.

Recall that with any inferential test, we are trying to use sample data to make an inference about the true state of things in the population. If we had data for the entire population, we could find the population correlation coefficient. The symbol for the population correlation coefficient is ρ, the Greek letter "rho." Researchers seldom have access to population data, so we must make use of sample data instead. In this usual case, we use the sample correlation coefficient (r) as an estimate of the unknown population correlation coefficient.

Ultimately, our hypothesis is about ρ (the population correlation coefficient) and not the sample correlation coefficient (r). Just as with other statistical significance tests, we are more confident in our conclusion when the sample size is larger. Therefore, the larger our sample, the easier it is to conclude that there is a significant difference between ρ and zero. If the null hypothesis is rejected, the researcher can conclude something like "There is sufficient evidence to conclude that there is a significant linear relationship between X and Y because the correlation coefficient is significantly different from zero." This suggests that the regression line from the sample data provides a more informative model of Y given X. If the researcher fails to reject the null hypothesis, then it cannot be said that there is a high probability that the observed relationship really exists in the population. It follows that it is inappropriate to make statements about the regression line.

For any sample correlation, there are two competing hypotheses about the population correlation:

Null Hypothesis: $\rho = 0$

Alternate Hypothesis: $\rho \neq 0$

Several different methods can be used to determine the probability level associated with a particular correlation at a given sample size. The "old school" way to do it is via a table. For whatever reason, the Excel function doesn't provide a probability with Pearson's r. The easiest way to test the hypothesis in Excel is to use the regression procedure and evaluate the t-test probability, which will be identical to the p-value of t in Pearson's r. This works because both methods are a subset of the General Linear Model (GLM) and they really do the same thing.

Key Terms

Sample correlation coefficient, population correlation coefficient, General Linear Model (GLM)

Section 6.5:
ANOVA Tests

An obvious limitation of the t-test is that it can only test the differences between *two* means. Researchers often find that they need to utilize more than two groups, such as when a medical researcher wishes to have a placebo group and two or more other groups. The **one-way analysis of variance (ANOVA)** is designed for just such research situations. As with the t-tests, the one-way ANOVA results in a probability that can be used to evaluate the null hypothesis. This probability is based on what is known as an F statistic, and for this reason, ANOVA tests are sometimes known as F tests.

There are several steps along the way to getting to F. Traditionally, these steps are presented in an **ANOVA summary table.** An ANOVA Table presents the source of variation (between groups, within groups, and total), the degrees of freedom for that source, the sum of squares for that source, the mean square for that source, and finally an F statistic. The level of significance is often presented as an ANOVA table footnote.

Figure 35. ANOVA Table with Component Abbreviations.

Source of Variation	df	Sum of Squares	Mean Square	F
Between Groups	df_b	SS_B	MS_B	?*
Within Groups	df_w	SS_W	MS_W	
Total	df_t	SS_T		

*p =?

Post Hoc Tests

In a case where only a single mean difference is examined, both F and t will lead the researcher to the same conclusion. When there are more than two groups and thus more than a single comparison, F evaluates whether the *set* of differences is statistically significant. If we determine that a particular F is statistically significant, we have the problem of not knowing which particular pairs of means are statistically significant. This problem is solved by conducting **multiple comparison tests**. Over the years, researchers have developed many multiple comparison tests (also known as *post hoc* tests). Each is an attempt to deal with the problem of the probability of making an error increasing with each new test. The researcher only conducts the post hoc tests if the overall F is found to be significant.

Computing the One-way ANOVA Test

To compute the value of F for a one–way ANOVA, use the following equation:

$$F = \frac{MS_B}{MS_w}$$

Where:
- F is the ANOVA test statistic
- MS_B is the Mean Square between groups
- MS_W is the Mean Square within groups

To obtain the values necessary to compute F, you must first compute the *total sum of squares* (SS_T). Do this using the following formula:

$$SS_T = \sum X^2 - \frac{(\sum X_T)^2}{N}$$

Where
- $\sum X^2$ is the sum of the squared scores for each group
- $\sum X_T$ is the sum of all scores
- N is the total number of subjects

To compute the *between groups sum of squares* (SS_B), use the following formula:

$$SS_B = \sum \frac{(\sum X)^2}{n} - \frac{(\sum X_T)^2}{N}$$

Where
- $\frac{(\sum X)^2}{n}$ is the sum of the X scores for each group squared divided by the number of subjects in each group. *This must be computed for each group and then added together.*
- And ($\sum X_T$) is the sum of all of the scores squared

To compute the within groups sum of squares (SS_W), use the following formula:

$SS_W = SS_T - SS_B$

Each term in the ANOVA table must have its degrees of freedom computed:
- df_b: subtract 1 from the number of groups
- df_t: subtract 1 from the total number of subjects
- df_w: subtract the degrees of freedom between from the degrees of freedom total

To compute the mean squares (MS), divide each sum of squares by its degrees of freedom.

Computing the Probability of F in Excel

To compute the probability of *F* using Excel, use the **FDIST** function.

Figure 36. Computing p for *F* in Excel.

	Clipboard			Font		
	C6		▼	f_x =FDIST(C3,C4,C5)		
	A	B	C	D	E	
1						
2						
3		F:	10.838			
4		DF (between):	2			
5		DF (within):	15			
6		Probability:	0.001224			
7						
8						
9						
10						
11						
12						
13						
14						

If you want to get a complete ANOVA table, you must use the **ANOVA: Single Factor** tool. In the data analysis ToolPak.

Figure 37. ANOVA in Excel.

		ID	Experimental	Control		Mean Difference =	1.800					
		1	8	7		N =	20.000					
		2	9	7		df =	18.000					
		3	7	4		t =	2.475					
		4	8	6		p =	0.023492					
		5	6	4								
		6	7	5		Anova: Single Factor						
		7	5	3								
		8	4	3		SUMMARY						
		9	7	6		Groups	Count	Sum	Average	Variance		
		10	9	7		Experimental	10	70	7	2.666667		
	SUM		70.00	52.00		Control	10	52	5.2	2.622222		
	Mean		7.00	5.20								
	SD		1.63	1.62								
						ANOVA						
						Source of Variation	SS	df	MS	F	P-value	F crit
						Between Groups	16.2	1	16.2	6.12605	0.023492	4.413873
						Within Groups	47.6	18	2.644444			
						Total	63.8	19				

Post Hoc tests

When the results of an ANOVA are significant, it tells us that at least one pair of means in the analysis is significantly different from another. The problem with this type of analysis is that it does not tell us which mean differences are significant. Post hoc tests are a family of tests that allow us to compare every mean with every other mean to determine which ones are significantly different.

You may wonder why we do not just conduct a t-test for each possible mean comparison and see which ones are significant. The problem with this is what researchers call an **inflated Type I error rate**. Recall that a Type I error means rejecting the null hypothesis when it is true, and the probability of this is specified by our alpha level. Therefore, if the researcher sets alpha at .05, then a Type I error will happen about 5% of the time. If we conduct 20 such tests, then the odds are very high that one of the tests will result in a Type I error. If we want our overall chance of a Type I error to remain at 5% for the entire analysis, we must adjust the probability of each comparison such that they sum to 5% and do not *each* have a 5% chance of error.

Type I Error Rate

A Type I error refers to a situation where a researcher rejects the null hypothesis when it is true.

The researchers selected alpha level establishes the level of acceptable risk.

This may seem like a small matter until we consider just how many comparisons there may be. The number of comparisons goes up very quickly as the number of groups increases. For example, when there are only two means, there is only one comparison. When there are three groups, there are three possible comparisons. With four groups, there are six possible comparisons. With five groups, there are ten possible comparisons. To deal with the inflated Type I error rate caused by all of these comparisons, we must use a special significance test that takes the inflation into account. **Post hoc** tests do just that.

Post hoc tests *are a family of related statistical procedures used to test the significance of individual mean differences after an ANOVA test result is found to be statistically significant.*

Tukey's Test

Perhaps the most common method of controlling Type I error rates is using a test called the **Tukey Honestly Significant Difference (HSD).** The Tukey HSD is based on a variation of the t distribution that takes the number of means being compared into account. This distribution is called the *studentized range distribution* (See Appendix E for a table of critical values).

Computing Tukey's HSD Test

To compute HSD, use the following formula:

$$HSD = q\sqrt{\dfrac{MS_W}{n}}$$

Where:

    q = the standardized range statistic (obtained from Appendix E)

    MS_W = The mean square for within groups from the ANOVA

    n = the number of subjects in each group (all groups must be of equal size)

Once we obtain a value for HSD, we simply compare it to the observed difference between the means. If the observed difference between a pair of means is larger than HSD, we reject the null hypothesis. Of the observed difference between a pair of means is smaller than HSD, we fail to reject the null hypothesis.

Unfortunately, Excel does not support post hoc tests, although it will produce an ANOVA table with relative ease. A researcher conducting an ANOVA can produce those results in Excel, then make post hoc comparisons using the simple formula above.

Suppose that a researcher has three groups in an experiment and he runs a one-way ANOVA in Excel to get the following results:

Figure 38. One-way ANOVA Results.

A	B	C	Anova: Single Factor							
8	4	3								
6	7	3	SUMMARY						Mean Differences	
5	4	1	Groups	Count	Sum	Average	Variance		A v. B	0.500
8	7	3	A	6	37	6.167	3.767		A v. C	3.667
3	5	4	B	6	34	5.667	2.267		B v. C	3.167
7	7	1	C	6	15	2.5	1.5			
			ANOVA							
			Source of Variation	SS	df	MS	F	P-value	F crit	
			Between Groups	47.44444	2	23.72222	9.446903	0.002212	3.68232	
			Within Groups	37.66667	15	2.511111				
			Total	85.11111	17					

Note the Mean Differences table within Figure 38. This is not produced by the ANOVA function in Excel; it must be set up by the researcher using simple subtraction. We know from the ANOVA that at least one of the mean differences is significant, but we do not know which one. To find out, we can conduct post hoc tests. To do this, we must find the value for HSD for each possible comparison (in this example, there are 3).

To use the formula for HSD, we must first consult the table in Appendix E and find the value of q. To do this, we consult the ANOVA summary table and find the degrees of freedom for *within groups*. We consult the table and find where 15 degrees of freedom meets with 3 groups. The value of q, then, is 3.67. We can then plug these values into the HSD formula:

$$HSD = 3.67\sqrt{\frac{2.511}{6}} = 2.374$$

For the comparison A v. B, the observed difference was 0.500. Since 0.500 is *not* greater than 2.374, we fail to reject the null hypothesis. In other words, the difference between Group A and Group B is *not* statistically significant.

For the comparison A v. C, the observed difference was 3.667. Since 3.667 is larger than 2.374, we reject the null hypothesis. In other words, the difference between Group A and Group C is statistically significant.

For the comparison B v. C, the observed difference was 3.167. Since 3.167 is larger than 2.374, we reject the null hypothesis. In other words, the mean difference between Group A and Group B is statistically significant.

The Tukey test is one among a field of many post hoc tests, but it is probably the most commonly encountered.

Two-Way ANOVA Tests

The one-way ANOVA has a single independent variable (IV) which is usually a grouping variable, such as when an experimenter has a placebo and one or more experimental groups. The **two-way ANOVA** allows for two independent variables. In addition to examining the effect of the two factors, we can also examine the interaction of the two factors using the two-way ANOVA.

Each *way* in an ANOVA is a grouping variable. Thus, a two-way ANOVA means that the subjects are classified by two variables, rather than by the one grouping variable in the one-way ANOVA. The ways are also known as *factors*. The effect of one grouping variable while not taking the other into account is known as a **main effect**. With the two-way ANOVA, there are two main effects.

Sometimes, the main effect of one independent variable will depend on the level of the other dependent variable. When this is the case, the two variables are said to have an **interaction**.

Key Terms

one-way analysis of variance (ANOVA), F statistic, ANOVA summary table, multiple comparison tests, post hoc tests, Type I error rate, Tukey Honestly Significant Difference (HSD), two-way ANOVA, main effect, interaction effect

Chapter 7:
Complex Models

So far, we have considered statistical methods that consider only one (univariate) or two variables (bivariate) at a time. The problem with this is that *the social world is* **multivariate** *in nature.* That is, the causes of the social phenomena that social scientists are interested in studying are many. Take for example a researcher interested in sentencing disparities based on race. The relationship between race and sentence length could be examined (assuming that accurate data can be obtained), but this picture would be far from complete unless the seriousness of the offense was taken into account. If the researcher were to include the seriousness of the offense and the race of the defendant, then a more complete picture will emerge. The relative effects of both variables can be examined.

Our last chapter, then, considers statistical techniques that consider sets of variables and how different sets of variables relate to each other as sets. Because there are more than two variables involved, these methods are usually classified as **multivariate statistics**. We will stay away from the complex mathematics necessary to obtain the results of these methods. Our concern will be with the logic of particular methods, the assumptions, and the interpretation of results. The hope is that when you finish this chapter, you will be able to read and interpret the social scientific literature that presents the results of these methods.

Students: *If you are using this book for an undergraduate course, pay special attention to your professor's instructions regarding this material. It may be considered too advanced, and you may not have time to cover it in a single term. You will most likely be assigned parts of this material rather than all of it. If you are a graduate student, then most likely you will have to master all of the concepts in this section.*

Section 7.1:
Multiple Regression

Previously, we learned that regression analysis can be used to predict the value of a variable Y given the value of a variable X. This is obviously a very useful tool for the social scientist attempting to explain, predict, and control social phenomena. A problem with this is that most social phenomena are very complex, and one predictor variable rarely does a very good job of predicting an outcome variable. Most social phenomena have multiple causes, and a mathematical model of those phenomena should consider multiple contributing factors. This deficiency is partially solved by *multiple linear regression*.

Multiple regression analysis is a statistical tool that allows the researcher to use two or more independent variables (Xs) to predict a single dependent variable (Y). Like the simple linear regression technique we learned earlier, multiple regression assumes that the relationship between X and Y is linear for all Xs.

> **Multiple Regression** is a statistical technique that allows for the prediction of a single dependent variable Y with multiple independent variables.

Adam J. McKee

What Are Linear Models?

Perhaps the most basic element of social scientific inquiry is the search for cause and effect relationships. That is, for one reason or another, we want to be able to explain why some phenomenon (usually a human behavior) happens. Of course, our reverence and respect for the scientific method causes complications. Social scientists tend to avoid the terms "cause and effect" and prefer to talk about the Independent Variable (IV) and Dependent Variable (DV), or we simply say that the two (or more) variables of interest are "correlated."

Let us for a few moments consider something of a philosophical abstraction: What does it take to make a causal statement that social scientists can respect as rigorous and valid? The most common way to talk about these things is to symbolize the thing doing the causing (the IV) as "X." The thing being caused (the DV) is symbolized as "Y." While the average researcher wouldn't be so crass as to come out and say it, the point of the researcher's efforts is to demonstrate that **X** causes **Y**. For this statement to meet social scientific rigor, we must demonstrate **temporal precedence**. Temporal precedence is just a $64,000 word meaning that X comes before (precedes) Y in time. This is a built-in element of a true experiment: The researcher knows the cause ("treatment" in an experiment) comes before the outcome that is measured (the DV) because the treatment was manipulated by the researcher.

Researchers can (ideally) establish temporal precedence by experimental design (e.g., by conducting a true experiment). Another method is to use logic. This usually requires that a well-accepted theory be employed to refute the possibility that Y causes X. A researcher, for example, could advance an argument that balls being hit by bats is what causes them to fly out of the park. We would reject the alternative thesis that balls flying out of the park causes them to be hit by bats. The latter statement is judged invalid because it goes against our knowledge of physics, and on a more visceral level, it goes against a lifetime of empirical observations.

Another requirement of a causal statement is that some variable outside of our consideration is actually doing the causing, and it just seems like X causes Y. In our research, we often consider variables as closed systems; we are only worried about X and Y. We often do not consider Z and have not measured it. Since it hasn't been considered or measured, we didn't include it in any of our analyses. Consider what happens if Z and X are related (correlated) such that when Z goes up, X also goes up. Let us further suppose that Z and Y are correlated such that when Z goes up, Y goes up (and vice versa). If we observe only X and Y without the benefit of Z, we note that whenever X goes up, Y also goes up. They are correlated. It would be wrong to conclude, however, that X causes Y.

Interpreting Regression Results

Let us say for example that a statistics professor is required to give a departmental final exam to his students. All students taking statistics must take this final exam as a matter of policy. Our professor is concerned that the material he teaches and tests on his other exams may not adequately prepare students for the department-wide final exam. To test this, he uses regression analysis to see how well his test scores relate to the final scores. The figure below represents a multiple regression analysis of whether two tests can predict the value of scores on a final exam.

Regression coefficients are numbers that represent the change in Y for each unit change in X, taking the effects of all the other Xs into account. These are also known as **partial regression coefficients**. In simple regression, this is the slope of the line. In multiple regression, there is an analogous coefficient for every value of X.

Multiple R is the strength of the relationship between the cluster of predictor variables (the overall model) with Y. Its magnitude is interpreted in a similar way to r. R^2 is the coefficient of determination for the overall model. It basically tells how closely the regression line describes the real data points. If R^2 is 1.0, then the line describes the data perfectly. Any downward departure from 1.0 indicates that the equation does an imperfect job of describing the actual data. Because it measures the "fit" of the line to the actual data, R^2 is often referred to as a **goodness of fit** measure. In our hypothetical example, our professor can rest easy knowing that most of the variance in final exam scores can be explained by how well students did on his Test 1 and Test 2. He can reasonably infer from this that the material he is covering is indeed preparing students.

Figure 39. Multiple Regression Results in Excel.

	A	B	C	D	E	F
1	SUMMARY OUTPUT					
2						
3	*Regression Statistics*					
4	Multiple R	0.96335355				
5	R Square	0.928050062				
6	Adjusted R Square	0.912061187				
7	Standard Error	2.315306336				
8	Observations	12				
9						
10	ANOVA					
11		*df*	*SS*	*MS*	*F*	*Significance F*
12	Regression	2	622.3008758	311.1504	58.04348715	0.0000
13	Residual	9	48.24579085	5.360643		
14	Total	11	670.5466667			
15						
16		*Coefficients*	*Standard Error*	*t Stat*	*P-value*	
17	Intercept	32.01836159	4.369055126	7.328441	0.0000	
18	Test 1	0.398154918	0.065646513	6.065134	0.0002	
19	Test 2	0.247527417	0.052160272	4.745516	0.0011	
20						

Another way to think of this is to consider the regression equation as a mathematical **model** of reality. The purpose of any model, such as a model airplane, is to mimic the essential characteristics of something but with less complexity than the thing being modeled. In social research, we use statistical models to approximate how a social phenomenon works. Regression statistics help us evaluate how good of a job our model does at approximating reality. If R^2 is equal to one, then it perfectly describes the phenomenon (at least in our sample data). Because human behavior is so complex, we rarely achieve that level of descriptive and predictive power.

The regression results also provide what is known as an Overall F Test, or simply an **ANOVA table**. The ANOVA test evaluates the statistical significance of the overall model, not the individual predictors. We interpret the probability of this ANOVA as we did previously. Since the significance is less than .05 and .01, we can conclude that at least one of the predictor variables is significantly related to the final test score. The relevant null and alternative hypotheses can be stated as follows:

H_0: There is no statistically significant relationship between the dependent variable Y and the set of independent variables (Xs).

H_1: There is a linear relationship between the dependent variable Y and at least one of the independent variables (Xs).

The ANOVA test evaluates the overall model. To examine the significance of particular independent variables, we use the associated t-test. A t-test is reported for each predictor variable. The test evaluates the hypothesis that there is a linear relationship between X and Y when holding all the other predictor variables constant. Another way to look at it is that the t-test evaluates whether adding a predictor adds any predictive power to a model that already has the other variables in place.

Let us say you develop a regression model that has a person's weight measured in pounds as a predictor variable. You accidentally add the person's weight measured in kilograms to the model. With weight measured in pounds already in the model, t would not be significant because it contains the exact same information that is already in the model, so adding weight in kilograms adds nothing to the predictive power of the model. For an individual value of t to be significant, the relevant variable must make a unique contribution to the predictive power of the regression equation.

Examine the diagram below. Its purpose is to illustrate how two predictor variables (X_1 and X_2) share variance (covary) with a dependent variable Y. Note that both predictors share some variance in common with both each other and Y, and that some of the variance of each predictor is only shared with Y and not the other predictor. The variance shared only between X_1 and Y is what the t-test for X_1 evaluates. Likewise, the t-test for X_2 evaluates the unique contribution of X_2 in predicting Y.

Figure 40.   Diagram of Shared Variance in Regression.

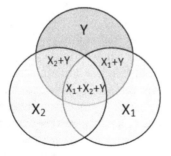

The multiple regression equation is identical to the equation we used with simple regression other than the fact that we add an additional term for each predictor variable:

$$\hat{Y} = a + b_1 X_1 + b_2 X_2 + b_3 X_3$$

In the above equation, the symbol $\hat{Y}$ is the predicted value of Y, and a is the **intercept** or **constant**. The coefficient b_1 is the regression coefficient for predictor variable X_1, b_2 is the regression coefficient for predictor variable X_2, and b_3 is the predictor variable for X_3. To predict a value for a particular set of X values, simply plug them into the formula along with the appropriate values for the intercept a and the regression coefficients b for each X.

Running a Multiple Regression in Excel

The multiple regression function in Excel is no different than that we used to run a simple regression analysis (only one predictor variable) other than we are highlighting a range of columns rather than a single column for X. The predictor variables must be adjacent columns. If they are not entered that way, then you can simply cut and paste them into a new sheet to get the layout you want. The first cell in every column can be a label. This makes interpreting your results much easier.

Examining Data

If you've ever taken a computer science class, you probably remember the oft-repeated adage "Garbage In, Garbage Out." This idea is critically important to the social scientific endeavor in general, and to regression analysis in particular. The quality of your research product will be directly proportionate to the quality of your data. (This is so important, in fact, that I recommend that you take a measurement class if at all possible before completing your graduate studies. You will learn all about topics like reliability and validity that make for excellent quality research).

Before you can use (ordinary least squares) regression analysis, it is important to determine if your X variables are related to your Y variables in a linear way. That is, does a straight line do a good job of describing the relationship? This basic assumption can be violated when there is no relationship between the variables (a terrible thing if you hypothesized such a relationship), or when there is a relationship that is better described by a curved line (or a complicated bendy line). Perhaps the easiest way to verify a linear relationship is to produce a simple scatterplot that shows X and Y for each ordered pair. If you do this in excel, you can also generate a prediction equation and fit a line to those points. Note that in the social sciences, we usually call the line the "regression line." In econometrics (and this in Excel) it is called a "trend line." It is the same thing.

Another important concept in regression analysis is the idea of **multicollinearity** (aka collinearity). Remember that a major purpose of regression analysis is to partition variance and ascribe the degree of relatedness in the DV. If there is a high correlation between the individual predictor (X) variables, then regression has no way to know how much "credit" to give each X in "causing" changes in Y. In other words, *multicollinearity* exists when two or more of the predictors in a regression model are moderately or highly correlated. Unfortunately, when it exists, it can wreak havoc on our analysis and thus limit the research conclusions that the researcher can draw. Specifically, it can cause a host of problems, including:

- the estimated regression coefficient of any one variable depends on which other predictors are included in the model
- the precision of the estimated regression coefficients decreases as more predictors are added to the model
- the marginal contribution of any one predictor variable in reducing the error sum of squares depends on which other predictors are already in the model
- hypothesis tests may yield different conclusions depending on which predictors are in the model

Note that collinearity is not a binary option, but a continuum from "very little" to "a huge amount"; often there will be a small degree of relatedness between the different X variables, but we can safely ignore *small* relationships. It is when we observe a moderate to high degree of interrelatedness that we grow concerned. Simply put, a little bit of collinearity is okay, but if it's a lot, then we have to do something about it.

One potential solution for this annoying problem is to design our research (specifically our measurements) such that our predictor variables are not related. Say, for example, we decide to conduct a study of college success using students' GPA after eight semesters as our DV. If we operationalize "preparedness" by using both ACT and SAT scores, we will likely run into a wall of collinearity because ACT scores and SAT scores are likely to be highly related (because they purport to measure very similar things). The cautious researcher would predict this relationship "muddying the waters" and choose to use only one such measure (or use a more advanced technique that takes collinearity into account, such as SEMs).

Multicollinearity happens more often than not in observational studies. And, unfortunately, regression analyses most often take place on data obtained from observational studies. (Most social scientific studies are observational because of ethical constraints). If you aren't convinced, flip through the pages of the latest issue of your favorite journal. You will most likely find that "true experiments" are a rarity. It is for this reason that we need to fully appreciate the sway of multicollinearity on our regression analyses.

To complicate things even further, we have to consider two different types of collinearity. The first is **Structural multicollinearity**. This type of collinearity occurs when there is a mathematical artifact caused by creating new predictors from other predictors (e.g., by data transformations)—such as, creating the predictor X^2 from the predictor X. If you have to have a problem, then this is a good one. You caused it, so you can fix it be tweaking your data file.

Data-based multicollinearity, on the other hand, is often a result of a poorly designed experiment, which can be very difficult to fix after the data are collected. This malady is also caused by reliance on purely observational data, or the lack of ability to manipulate the system on which the data were collected. Because data-based multicollinearity is usually a design issue, you should give your variables careful consideration in the design phase of your study.

The best way to deal with collinearity issues is to eliminate them through intelligent and parsimonious experimental designs rather than statistical control.

Transforming Data

Recall the idea of a **best-fit line**. The best fit line is most commonly drawn (such as in Excel) using a set of equations that assume that the line will be straight. Because of this mathematically dictated assumption, a basic assumption of ordinary least squares regression is that the relationships between X and Y are best described by a straight line. Sometimes, data that are not well described by a straight line can be "tweaked" to fit a straight line using **transformations**. Data transformations can also make data "cleaner" by shifting skewed distributions to become more symmetrical.

More formally, then, *transformation* is the replacement of a variable by a function of that variable. For example, replacing a variable X by the square root of x or the logarithm of X. The purpose of such a transformation is a replacement that changes the shape of a distribution or relationship.

A common transformation is the **log transformation**. A log transformation of raw data points brings the score for everyone in the dataset closer together for the transformed score. Because of the "magic of compounding," a straight line often does a poor job of describing things that happen as a percentage gain over time, such as populations in a particular place (or organization) or money in your retirement account. If we take the log of the population value, then a straight line often does do a good job of describing the data.

A very common reason for conducting a transformation is simply **convenience**. In other words, a transformed scale may be as natural (that is, provides for an intuitive interpretation) as the original scale and more convenient for an explicit purpose (e.g. percentages rather than original data). One common example in statistics is **standardization**, whereby scores are adjusted for differing level and spread. Standardized values have a mean of zero and a spread (usually expressed as standard deviation units) 1 and have no units. Therefore, standardization is useful for comparing variables expressed in different scales. (Most commonly a standard score is calculated using the mean and standard deviation (SD) of a variable).

It is important to note that standardization makes no difference to the shape of a distribution. That is, a skewed distribution of scores will remain skewed when standardized. Most of the transformation made for convenience sake are convenient because they remove confusion caused by scales and provide a "pure" number that has an intuitive interpretation. This is the same reason educators most often report grades to students as a percentage rather than a number of correct answers—we all know what a grade of 85% means intuitively. Standardized scores are the same way for researchers; we all have been trained to think in the metric of z-scores. Educators would be just as comfortable if you converted those scores to GPA units. Psychologists that do a lot of testing are equally familiar with T-scores.

Another important reason that researchers often transform data is to reduce skewness. A distribution that is symmetrical (or nearly so) is often easier to "handle" and interpret than a skewed distribution. More specifically, a normal or Gaussian distribution is often desirable because it is a fundamental assumption of many statistical methods. The assumptions of statistical tests are critically important to the researcher because **the results of statistical tests are only accurate if the assumptions are met**. To reduce right skewness, take roots or logarithms or reciprocals (roots are generally regarded as the weakest transformation method). To reduce left skewness, take squares or cubes or higher powers.

Another reason that researchers employ transformations is to "equalize spreads." Each data set or subset having about the same spread or variability is a condition called **homoscedasticity**. This condition of "similar spreadoutness" is desirable because it is an important assumption of many statistical tests. The opposite condition is called **heteroscedasticity**. **Heteroscedastic** data is a problem because it violates the homoscedasticity requirement of many statistical tests.

When looking at relationships between variables, it is often far easier to think about patterns that are approximately linear than about patterns that are highly curved. **Linearity**, then, is vitally important when using linear regression, which amounts to fitting a straight line to data points. For example, a scatterplot of the logarithms of a series of values against time usually has the property that periods with constant rates of change plot as straight lines. The raw data, on the other hand, will tend to be curved.

Creating **additive relationships** is another reason that researchers transform data. Additive relationships are often easier to analyze when additive rather than multiplicative (or some other transformation). For example, our basic and beloved simple regression equation $Y' = a + bX$ is much easier to interpret than a multiplicative model such as $Y' = aX^b$. In other words, it may be better to use a data transformation to eliminate the curve rather than to explicitly model the curve.

In practice, a transformation often works, serendipitously, to accomplish several of these purposes at once, particularly to reduce skewness, to produce nearly equal variances, and to produce a nearly linear (or additive) relationship. It is important to note that this fortuitous state of affairs is not guaranteed. Often, the best solution to choosing a transformation is to examine the raw scores to see if a line does a good job. If not, then you can try various transformations to see if the fit improves. The main criterion in choosing a transformation is *what works with the data*. It is important to consider two other questions:

1. What makes sense to researchers and consumers of research in the field?

2. Can the researcher keep dimensions and units simple and convenient?

If possible, prefer measurement scales that are easy to think about. Often, however, somewhat complicated units are a sacrifice that has to be made so that statistical assumptions can be met. When lack of linearity is the problem, an alternative idea is to model the curve, but this only works well if there are only a couple of "bends" in the line.

Statistical Inference and Regression

The idea of statistical inference is closely related to the idea of what has been called Null Hypothesis Significance Testing (NHST). While controversial in elite research circles, these sorts of tests are ubiquitous in the literature across the social science disciplines. In the first course in statistics, most students learn to think of the decision reject or fail to reject *the* null hypothesis as the primary objective. In the world of multivariate statistics, there may be several such evaluations rather than a single one. Recall how the two-way ANOVA works; there are really three hypotheses. There are two factors, each with a hypothesis that must be evaluated, plus the interaction effect. That is the sort of idea we are considering here.

Let's think back to our previous discussions for a few minutes and reconsider exactly what all this hypothesis testing stuff is about. The first thing that we must recall is that all this stuff is worthless if you have census data. We only need inferential statistics when we want to make inferences about a population using *sample* data. The problem with samples is that they sometimes don't do a very good job of representing the population like we want them to do. You probably remember from a research methods class that bad sampling techniques can lead to samples that do a terrible job of reflecting the characteristics of the population being studied. If that is the case, then the results of our study will be useless.

That is, in essence, a research design issue, and a reminder of our mantra "garbage in, garbage out." The other source of bad samples that don't reflect the population we are trying to study is random chance—called **sampling error**. Recall that in this context "error" doesn't mean we did anything bad; there is no pejorative connotation. Anything statisticians can't explain is called "error." In every sample, we even expect a little error. Because randomly occurring errors tend to be normally distributed, we can do a pretty good job of estimating how much error is likely in a given sample.

Your statistics professor probably beat you over the head with *mean differences* for months, causing some degree of trauma and a deep-seated misconception that hypotheses and null hypotheses are all about means. We need to expand that idea. Keep in mind that any characteristic of a population—called a **parameter**—can be estimated using sample data. Not only can we estimate means, but we can extend that idea to standard deviation, variances, covariances, and ultimately regression coefficients. Statistical hypothesis tests help us determine of obtaining a particular parameter estimate by chance (due to sampling error) is small enough to be disregarded.

Recall that researchers specify the chance they are willing to take of being wrong in disregarding chance by setting an **alpha level**. Conventionally, alpha is set at .05 or .01 (as an artifact of statistical table construction; today you are strongly advised to report *actual* probabilities). This means that the researcher is specifying that she is willing to accept a 5% chance or a 1% chance of wrongly rejecting chance (randomly generated sampling error) when it is, in fact, the cause of the observed parameter.

The above statements were necessarily vague because those "parameters" can be anything you wish to calculate. In t-tests, we learned that the parameter of interest was the difference between means. If we saw such a difference in the sample, were left to wonder if it really existed in the population, or whether we just had a wonky sample that made it *appear* that the treatment worked. That's what our hypothesis test does—and *all it does*. To go beyond excluding wonky samples, you have to consider effect size and how meaningful a particular effect size is in your particular research context.

It is beyond the scope of this little book to examine thoroughly, but know that NHST is highly controversial in more sophisticated research circles. Conversely, they have been the bread and butter of social and behavioral researchers for a century, and the literature is full of them. The modern researcher will nearly always find herself in the middle of this debate. My suggestion? Straddle the fence by considering both effect size and power in your design.

Testing the Regression of Y on X

Recall that most statistical significance tests end up being a *variance ratio* in the end. I call these "signal to noise" ratios; they are proxies for explained variance over unexplained variance. In regression, we can compute a quantity known as the **regression sum of squares** (SS_{reg}). That is the "signal"—the explained variance— just like the numerator in the F equation you used in a one-way ANOVA calculation as an undergraduate. You can also compute a residual sum of squares (SS_{res}). In regression, residuals are the difference between the *predicted* value of Y and the *actual* value of Y in the sample data.

If X does a great job of predicting Y, then residuals will be very small. If X doesn't do a very good job of predicting Y, then the residuals will be quite large. So, if we consider the ratio of the regression sum of squares over the residual sum of squares, we get a "signal to noise" ratio just like with an F test. When we adjust that for the degrees of freedom for each quantity, it actually becomes an F test, and we evaluate it just like we do the results of a one-way ANOVA test. The null hypothesis for these ANOVA results is that there is no relationship between X and Y. In its simplest form, this can be thought of as $r = 0.00$.

Testing R^2

Recall that r^2 indicates the proportion of variance of the DV accounted for by the IV. We can infer from this simple relationship that $1 - r^2$ is the proportion of variance of the DV not accounted for by the IV. Pedhazur (1997) demonstrates that this later quantity is also the proportion of error variance. He goes on to provide an equation for F based on values of R2 rather than the sum of squares (p. 29). This version of the computation is much more intuitive because it suggests that it is R2 that is being tested. In this context, we can infer that the null hypothesis is that R^2 = 0.00, or that the specified model (combination of X values) has no explanatory power of the variance in Y. In computer-generated regression outputs, there will commonly be an ANOVA table. This is the test produced in that table—it is a significance test of the overall regression model as represented by R^2.

Testing Regression Coefficients

As a multivariate tool, multiple regression produces an overall test of the specified model, and it also produces individual coefficients for each X variable in the model. Like other statistics, the regression coefficient, b, has a standard error associated with it. This is the "noise" component that allows us to construct a statistical significance test using the "signal to noise ratio" format that we've previously considered. The null hypothesis is essentially that b = 0.0. (It can also test whether b differs significantly from any hypothesized value, but this is rarely seen in the literature). Most researchers find that the t-distribution is better for this purpose, so regression coefficients (b) are usually evaluated with a t-statistic that has an associated probability. If that probability falls below your alpha level, then you reject the null hypothesis.

Variance Partitioning

If you want to get at the big idea of all inferential statistics, my answer would be "to partition variance." We know correlation and regression techniques can be used to talk about relationships and relatedness. Rarely, however, are those things the real goals of the social scientific endeavor. The goal of most science is to *explain social phenomena*. In this search for an explanation, we often attempt to identify variables (IVs) that affect the phenomenon we are trying to explain (the DV), but we also want to understand their relative importance. This quest boils down to two basic and related methods. The first is what we'll call variance partitioning. The other (which we'll consider in a later section) is the analysis of effects.

Recall that regression analysis can be used as an analytical tool in experimental, quasi-experimental, and descriptive research. The interpretation of regression results is far easier in experimental research because of the magic of random assignment. Still, regression methods can be used with those other types of research so long as due caution is used. I leave you with Elazar Pedhazur's (1997) sage advice in this regard: "*Sound thinking within a theoretical frame of reference, and a clear understanding of the analytic methods used are probably the best safeguard against drawing unwarranted, illogical, or nonsensical conclusions"* (p. 242).

Recall that R^2 (the coefficient of determination) can be interpreted as the proportion of variance in Y that is explained by knowing the value of a predictor X, or a set of predictors (X_1, X_2, X_3, and so forth). When we refer to "variance partitioning" we are really just talking about determining a proportion of R^2 that can be attributed to a *particular* X (or set of X values). In the simplest case where only one X is used to predict Y, this work is done for us. There is only one IV, so we can attribute all of R^2 to that variable.

Understanding variance partitioning in regression requires that we master new vocabulary. You will encounter these terms frequently in the literature, so learning them is a very good idea. The first term we want to consider is the idea of a **zero-order correlation**. The zero order correlation is the correlation of a particular X with Y with no other X values taken into account. You already know all about these— They are the same thing as Pearson's *r*.

One way to think of how we get R^2 in multiple regression (two or more IVs) is to add up the zero-order correlations. In other words, we could compute a Pearson's *r* for each *X*, square those, and then add them all up. That method will actually work if we stipulate that none of the *X* values are correlated with each other as well as Y. If they share variance with each other and Y, then R^2 must be reduced because the overlapping covariance can't be counted twice. If we do allow that same variance to be counted twice (or more), we can potentially end up with a highly inflated R^2 that vastly overestimates the predictive power of our model. We can also end up *with a nonsensical result such as explaining 125% of the variance in Y by knowing X_1, X_2, and X_3.* Logic dictates that we can't explain more than 100% (R^2 = 1.0) of the variance in Y.

Note that when we are entering regression models into computer software, *the order of entry is of critical importance.* This is because the first *X* that we enter into the model gets to "claim" all of the variance it shares with Y. In other words, if we enter X_1 first (which would be a logical default), we begin computing R^2 with the zero order correlation of X_1 with Y. For subsequent variables, the squared **semi-partial correlations** are used.

The takeaway from this is that when the IVs are at all intercorrelated, the proportion of variance attributed to each variable depends on its order of entry into the model. It is a mistake, then, to assume that one variable (especially the first) is more strongly associated with Y based on its contribution to R^2. This all means that we can be sure of R^2 because it does not change, regardless of the order entry of our predictor variables. The relative contribution of each *X*, however, can change dramatically. Unfortunately, there is no mathematical way to sort all this out. Some authors have gone so far as to suggest that the idea of an "independent contribution to variance" as meaningless when the predictors are intercorrelated. This has done little to remove the questionable practice from researchers' toolboxes and thus the professional literature. Always interpret an author's discussion of the results of a regression partitioning exercise with extreme caution.

Hierarchical Regression Analysis

One approach to variance partitioning is to use what has become known as **hierarchical regression analysis**, which has also been called *incremental partitioning of variance*. The idea is pretty simple: You dump all the variables in your study into a regression model. You get R^2 for that model. You then run the model again, adding your variable of interest. If your new variable contributes some new explanatory power, then R^2 will rise. (Any time two models are compared, you can examine the change in R^2. This "change" is often footnoted using the Greek letter delta: ΔR^2).

The logic is that such a rise indicates the "independent contribution" of that variable. Pedhazur (1997) warns against such an interpretation (p. 245). He does suggest, however, that such as method is perfectly fine when the researcher wants to examine the effect of the one variable while controlling for the effects of the others (we'll consider the idea of statistical control in a later section).   Simply put, *incremental partitioning of variance is not a valid way of determining the relative importance of a variable.*

Analysis of Effects

In statistics and research, when we use the term "effect" we are talking about the effect of an independent variable on a dependent variable. Similarly, when we talk about the "effect size" we are talking about the *magnitude* of the effect. Most of the language that social scientists use come from experimental research in medicine and psychology. In true experiments, the independent variable is manipulated by the researcher; such researchers are thus interested in *treatment effects*. Most of the time, they can examine the existence of a treatment effect using two basic methods (that are really a single method—the difference is language and vantage point).

The first method is to have an experimental group and a control group. The experimental group gets the treatment, and the control group gets a placebo (or the status quo treatment). One approach is to look at the mean differences between the experimental group and the control group. A difference in the means *suggests* that the treatment worked. One of the most widely used statistics to test such research designs is the **t-test**. Recall from your earlier statistics courses that t-tests are used when the independent variable is the grouping variable—in other words, the value of the independent variable for each participant is whether or not they got the treatment. Also, recall that we can expand this basic idea to look at more than two groups using the ANOVA designs.

You may never have considered exactly what *t* represented when you computed them in the past. (You needed to know what *t* was rather desperately, not what it means!). The computation of t is really just a ratio, expressed as a fraction. The top of the *t* equation is just the difference between the means. The bottom is just an estimate of the standard deviation in the difference between means distribution. That quantity gives us an estimation of about how much difference in means we can expect from purely random selection effects. So, t gives us a ratio of the observed effect from the experiment and the likely effects of random chance. In other words, it gives us a "signal to noise" ratio.

t = experimental difference / likely random chance difference (standard error of the differences)

If the chances are *equal* that the treatment worked and that random chance caused the observed differences, then we can't make any statements about the treatment working. It's just a coin toss. When the ratio starts to get bigger than one, we start to have more evidence that the effect was real and not due to random chance. We could (if we weren't trying to be scientific) draw arbitrary lines in the sand and specify how many times larger than the effect of chance we needed the observed (experimental) effect to be before we are willing to say that the treatment effect very likely worked and that random chance effects are very unlikely as an explanation of the experimental results (recall that such a statement is the idea of *statistical significance*). Thanks to the properties of the normal curve, we can draw statistical lines in the sand based on probabilities. These shift with the number of participants, which is why researchers like large sample sizes—the power of a statistical test increases as sample size increases. As you can see from the ratio that makes up t, the bigger the effect size, the bigger the ratio will be; this means that the bigger the effect size is, the easier it is to find statistical significance (reject the null hypothesis).

When we choose an alpha of .05, we are essentially specifying that if the observed difference is about twice the size of the likely difference due to chance (as estimated by the standard error), then we will reject the null hypothesis and conclude that the population means is not likely to be zero ($p < .05$).

Let's pause for a minute and clarify some terminology that may be different in "mean difference tests" and in regression analysis. As we previously stated, the independent variable has an "effect" on the dependent variable. If we make our analysis more complex, such as with a two-way ANOVA, then we'll have two different independent variables. This complicates the analysis because we have two *effects* to analyze. To make matters worse, since the two factors can interact, we have to examine ***interaction effects***. So, in the language of 'experimental designs,' we have two **main effects** and one **interaction effect** to analyze when we are doing a two-way ANOVA. Note that the two independent variables in such an analysis are known as **factors** in the language of experimental design. We can do some pretty complicated designs (given the right software) that go beyond the basic two-way ANOVA in complexity. These are considered under the heading of "factorial designs" in most experimental design textbooks. In the language of regression analysis, they are just called independent variables. The differences in terminology are historical accidents. When you understand the idea of the General Linear Model (GLM), the distinctions evaporate and understanding what is going on becomes merely a matter of keeping a bunch of synonyms straight.

When you hear the idea of an "effect" in regression analysis, you are usually dealing with someone steeped in the methods of experimental designs using regression analysis to analyze experimental results.

Note that a basic assumption of Pearson's *r* is that both the dependent variable and the independent variable are measured at least at the ratio level of measurement. This means you can't do a Pearson's *r* on experimental data because the IV (the grouping variable) is discrete—you are either in group 1 or group 2. Simple linear regression has the same limitation. However, brilliant mathematical statisticians figured out that if you **dummy code** the independent variables, everything works out okay. The way dummy coding works is simple; if a participant is in the category of interest, you score them as 1. If they are not in the category of interest, you score them as 0. For example, if a participant got the pill in a medical experiment, then you'd code them as 1. If they got the placebo, you'd code them as zero. You can also code naturally occurring categories like this, but you have to be careful the remember your coding scheme when you are analyzing results, so you know which category to attribute to what results. In other words, if you were interested in a gender effect, you could code female participants as 1, and then code male participants as 0.

Using dummy coding, then, you can get the exact same results and reach the exact same conclusions using regression as you would get using a t-test. In a regression analysis, *B* gives you the mean difference between the two groups. The standard error of *B* in the regression analysis is the same as the standard error in a t-test. And, of course, the value of *t* for the coefficient in a regression analysis is the same as the value of *t* in a regression analysis. The intercept in the regression analysis is the mean of the group that you coded zero. Think about the implications of that given the way the regression equation works. The predicted value of Y will be the intercept (the mean of the group you coded zero), and the slope of the line, which is *B*. *B* is the mean difference, so you get the mean of the group coded 1 by adding the mean difference to the mean of the other group. It makes perfect sense in the simple case of a binary (only two values, such as experimental and control group) independent variable. Note that if you code things the other way around, the results will stay the same, but the sign of **B** will reverse since the slope of the line will be going the other way.

I will not belabor the point here, but we can extend this logic to one-way ANOVA designs, two-way ANOVA designs, and unique models with mixed types of independent variables that fit our research situation.

Key Terms

multiple regression analysis, regression coefficients, partial regression coefficients, intercept, constant, R-square, dummy code

Adam J. McKee

Section 7.2:
Factor Analysis

I n social research, we are often interested in complex, **latent constructs** that cannot be directly observed. Imagine, for example, that a political scientist is interested in "conservatism." It would be a poor research project indeed of our researcher used the question "Are you a Democrat or a Republican?" to measure this variable. To really get at "conservatism," the researcher will need to include several facets of what it means to be a conservative. This would make the measure binary—you either are or are not conservative. Yet, most political scientists would agree that conservatism is a matter of degree. Some people are much more conservative than others are. There are also different aspects to the idea; there are foreign policy beliefs, religious beliefs, criminal justice beliefs, and economic beliefs (just to name a few) that factor into the concept. Now, back up and reread that last sentence, taking note of how the word "factor" is used. In this context, it means "a component" of something (*conservatism* in our example).

Factor analysis is a family of statistical methods that examine the degree of relatedness of measured variables thought to indicate a common, underlying construct.

We use the logic of these "factors" all the time; we just don't think about it on those exact terms. Let's say for example that your statistics professor gives you a quiz on central tendency that contains ten multiple choice questions. Her logic in doing so is not to see if you can answer those ten particular questions per se. The intent, rather, is to assess the underlying construct of "central tendency knowledge." Which questions she chose to use are based largely on professional judgment. The logic is that statistics professors are experts in statistics, and that expertise informs them as to what items are good measures of your knowledge of the material. But what if our professor is in a hurry and accidentally includes a question about variability? As a student, you would be upset. After all, you have not read the material on variability yet; you've studied central tendency. The question is not fair because it does not measure central tendency knowledge. To fix this problem, you would have to appeal to your professor's expertise again, hoping that she would judge the item not to measure the underlying construct that is was supposed to measure (and not include it in your grade).

In our statistics quiz example, the issue is simple. The construct *central tendency knowledge* is well defined, and it is relatively easy to see that an item concerning variability does not belong in the list of measured variables (test questions). In social science research, it is common for researchers to deal with constructs (factors) that are not so well understood and easily quantified. **Factor analysis** provides a method of judging how well a group of items (e.g., questions) is related. The logic is very simple: If we measure the same thing several different ways, then all of those measurements should be highly correlated. Factor analysis can also help us figure out how many underlying constructs there are in a given set of data. Let's return to our political scientist studying *conservatism*.

After an extensive review of the literature, our scholar may identify 25 questions thought to measure *conservatism*. But is it best to consider all of these items to measure such a general construct as "conservatism?" Or would our researcher achieve more accurate results if the construct is broken down into subcategories such as "religious conservatism" and "fiscal conservatism?" Since the ideas are related, all of the items will be correlated. Factor analytic techniques will break out these subcategories for us, based on the correlations between the items.

What factor analysis does, then, is identify a cluster of measurements that have high correlations between all of the items in the cluster. The computer will cluster the items; the subjective process of identifying and naming those clusters is still up to the researcher. For example, our political scientist friend may find that items 3, 6, 9, and 27 form a cluster (factor). What the nature of that cluster is may or may not be apparent. The items must be examined from a theoretical perspective to provide meaning to the numerical results. If all of them obviously have to do with social spending, then the interpretation is easy. If no such relationship is apparent, then interpreting the results can be quite difficult.

Higher Order Factors

Once again, let us return to the hypothetical example of the political scientist researching *conservatism*. A factor analysis reveals (let us say) five distinct factors in the data (obtained from asking participants the 25 questions). For each of these factors, a **factor score** can be calculated (there are several ways of doing this). If we are correct in our theoretical assumption that there is a *single* construct that we have named *conservatism*, then all of those factor scores should result in a *single* factor when factor analyzed. If our theoretical speculation is confirmed and only one factor is identified, then we have strong support for the theoretical position that there is indeed a "thing" called conservatism, and our 25 items measure that thing. When we identify a factor composed of other factors, statisticians call this a **higher order factor**.

How Much Does A Factor Explain?

Showing that there is a relationship between variables is an important function of nearly every statistic that we have discussed throughout this text. We have conceptualized that general idea in several different ways; We have looked at effect sizes like Cohen's *d*, we've looked at correlations, and we've considered measures like R^2. When it comes to using factors in social research, it is useless to use a factor to explain something when a single variable does just as good a job (after all, every good social scientist aims for parsimony). When we want to get at how good of a job a factor does at explaining variance versus a single variable, we can examine a statistic known as an *eigenvalue*.

The **eigenvalue** is a measure of how much of the variance in the observed variables a factor explains. Any factor with an eigenvalue greater than one (1.00) explains more variance than a single observed variable does. Note that you cannot interpret an eigenvalue as you do R^2. The eigenvalue is one possible method of deciding which factors to retain and which ones to "throw out" because they do not contain enough information to be useful. The interpretation of factor analyses can be difficult because there are technically as many factors as there are variables entered into the analyses. They are always presented (by software and in the professional literature) in the order of how much variation they explain. Factors that explain very little of the variation are usually discarded.

Statistical software usually offers the researcher some flexibility in determining the number of factors to extract. There are exploratory methods that use statistical cut points (like specified eigenvalues). There are confirmatory methods that extract the number of factors that the researcher specifies. The correct strategy depends largely on the researcher's purpose rather than any sort of objectively "best" method.

Assessing Individual Variables

Factors, then, are composed of several measured variables. The strength of the relationship between each measured variable and the factor that contains it is assessed by a statistic called a **factor loading**. Factor loadings are easy to interpret because they are interpreted the same as standardized regression coefficients. Statistical software will produce a table with each factor forming a column, and each variable in rows. Each variable will have a factor loading on each factor, which is the value in the cell where the variables intersect the factors. In the professional literature, factor loadings below a certain cut point are often omitted, making the table easier to interpret. Also, the variables may be ordered such that factors are easily identified. That is, the variables with high loadings on a particular factor are clustered together.

So far, we have considered factor analysis as a method of examining underlying factors. It can also be used to evaluate individual variables. Applied researchers can test the ability of one variable to serve as a proxy for several. In other words, if an individual item correlates very highly with a particular factor, then that variable can be used as a "stand in" for the more complex, harder to measure variable. Factor analysis can also be used to see if a particular item belongs with the factor that the researcher believes it does. The validity and reliability of standardized instruments can be enhanced in this way.

Types of Factor Analytic Techniques

Statisticians have been arguing for many years over the nuances of different techniques for examining the interrelatedness of data points. There are many mathematically different strategies, such as Principle Component Analysis (PCA). Others include principal axis factor, maximum likelihood, generalized least squares, and unweighted least squares. An exploration of these is beyond the scope of this text. Just be aware of these names so that when you see them, you can know that it is a species of factor analysis. All of them are designed to result in a *simple structure*. **Simple structure** is statistician speak for a pattern of results where each variable loads highly onto one and only one factor. Simple structures are often achieved through a piece of mathematical wizardry known as **rotation**, and there are several methods of accomplishing this.

The table below represents a typical journal presentation of factor analysis:

TABLE 1
Equamax Rotated Component Matrix, Pate and Annan (1989) Data, *n* = 921

Item	Factor I	Factor II	Factor III	Factor IV
Q38 Fear: Robbery	.838			
Q39 Fear: Attack	.808			
Q40 Fear: Break in Home Absent	.767			
Q41 Fear: Break in Home Present	.744			
Q42 Fear: Steal Car	.735			
Q50 Police: Helpful		.790		
Q51 Police: Fair		.754		
Q49 Police: Polite		.735		
Q47 Police: Help Victims		.635		
Q48 Police: Keep Order		.629		
Q20 Problem: Robbery			.746	
Q19 Problem: Attacks			.743	
Q62 Problem: Broken Windows			.633	
Q61 Problem: Junk in Lots			.614	
Q18 Problem: Public Drinking			.602	
Q21 Neighbor: Shop if Sick				.738
Q23 Neighbor: Borrow Money				.736
Q10 Neighbor: Ask Favor				.687
Q22 Neighbor: Watch Home				.635
Q25 Neighborhood Cooperation				.568

NOTE: Item question numbers and variable names come from the original data set. Loadings less than .400 are not displayed to facilitate factor identification.

Note that the sequentially numbered questions have been reordered so that the heavy loadings on the salient factor are clustered together. This facilitates an easy interpretation of the table. Also, note that the rotation method is provided in the table title. The author has omitted factor loadings below a .400. This is why it appears that each question loads on one and only one factor. In reality, every question will likely have some factor loading value on every factor.

Problems to Watch For

Factor analysis is a strategy that relies on large sample sizes to produce accurate (stable) results. If sample sizes are very, very large, then the results will likely be accurate. The first major size limitation is that when the sample has less than ten scores per variable, computational problems arise. This forms a bare minimum sample size. For really accurate results, some researchers recommend upwards of 500 subjects. When determining the quality of factor analysis results, always look for large sample sizes.

Key Terms

latent construct, factor analysis, factor score, higher-order factor, eigenvalue, factor loading, rotation

Section 7.3:
Logistic Regression

So far, our discussion of regression has considered models where the dependent variable is measured at the interval or ratio level. **Logistic regression** (a.k.a. **logit regression**) allows us to use the same logic (but with different math) for research situations where the dependent variable is measured at the categorical level of measurement. The most common version of this is when the options are binary; that is, there are only two choices. These research situations arise in the social sciences often. Pass/fail, conviction/acquittal, and prison/probation are possible examples of such binary pairs of options. There are methods that extend this idea beyond two categories (e.g., multinomial logistic regression), but these are beyond the scope of this text.

In ordinary least squares regression (OLS Regression, the stuff we already talked about), the prediction equation is based on a combination of the effects of predictor variables. You can visualize as this as various pulls and pushes on a playground seesaw. Logistic regression uses a fundamentally different approach: In logistic regression, predictions are made looking at the probabilities (also referred to as odds) associated with a particular predictor. Not that I've used the term binary several times. **Binary**, you probably recall from a computer class, means information made up entirely of zeros and ones. Keep that idea in mind, and recall the levels of information we discussed way back in the first chapter. Remember the nominal level? Most of the time, the binary Y variable that we want to predict with logistic regression represents a state of something; we usually put that into our statistical software using zeros and ones rather than names. For example, a researcher could code "fail" as 1 and "pass" as zero.

In OLS regression, a linear equation is built using the relative influence of the X scores to predict the value of Y. In logistic regression, we are not predicting Y per se, but rather we are predicting the probability of *Y* taking on a specific state. You can think of the null hypothesis for such a test as being like a coin toss. With a true coin toss, the chance of the coin coming up tails is 50%. In a research situation, if the X variable is related to the probability of Y, then the odds start to move in a particular direction. This means that we have a better chance of predicting the value of Y given the value of X (this part, at least, is the same as OLS regression). This means that the underlying logic of OLS regression and logistic regression are very similar. The math behind the results, however, is very different.

In previous sections, we've considered how to analyze dichotomous independent variables (IVs) using the technique of dummy coding. Often, researchers want to answer questions about dependent variables that are also dichotomous. Logistic regression estimates the *probability* of an outcome. Using this method, DVs are coded as binary variables with a value of 1 representing the occurrence of a target outcome, and a value of zero representing its absence.

Why can't we use regular (OLS) Regression?

Applying OLS regression to dichotomous dependent variables is problematic for several reasons. A major reason is that it violates some important assumptions: The errors cannot be normally distributed, and they cannot have a constant variance. In addition, such a linear model does not confine the level of the variable to a valid, discrete category. That is, predicted values based on such a model would fall outside of the logical range of zero and one.

About the Distributions

In very technical and older literature, there was much talk of "logit and probit" models. Today, there isn't much talk of "probit" models, and the logit model is usually referred to in terms of "logistic regression." The two methods differ in their probability distributions. The big reason that probit models fell out of favor was that probit coefficients are essentially uninterpretable. They don't make "common sense" in any way. Most researchers prefer logistic regression because it results in coefficients that can be transformed into the familiar odds ratio by "exponentiating" the coefficient.

Adam J. McKee

About Odds Ratios

Often, novice researchers improperly interpret **odds ratios** as *probabilities*—this is wrong. The "odds" of an outcome occurring is a *ratio of successes to failures*. For example, an odds of 1.00 would correspond to a probability of 0.50. *Odds ratios*, then, reflect the predicted change in the odds given a 1 unit change in the predictor. That is, the odds ratio reflects change relative to the base odds of the outcome occurring. Given an outcome that either rarely occurs or almost always occurs, a *small* change in probability can correspond to a *large* odds ratio. Odds ratios are a ratio of ratios which can be quite confusing!

Because of this confusion, you will need to study the interpretation of odds ratios in depth. You will also need to be able to explain them to a nontechnical audience. In other words, we need to be able to translate statistical software output into an intuitive way to understand your research results. Much of social research has policy and practice implications. Practitioners may not understand the idea of an odds ratio. In an academic writing context, this means that you'll provide a table of odds ratios for your sophisticated readers, but you'll also want to provide an intuitive understanding in your conclusions.

How are they Different?

Unlike OLS regression, logistic regression does not try to predict the value of a numeric variable given a set of predictor variables. Instead, the output is a *probability* that the given input point belongs to a certain class. The central premise of logistic regression is the assumption that your "input space" can be separated into two regions (one for each class) by a straight line boundary.

Logistic regression does not make many of the key assumptions of linear regression that are based on ordinary least squares mathematics (e.g., linearity, normality, homoscedasticity, and measurement level).

- Logistic regression does *not* require a linear relationship between the dependent and independent variables. It can handle all sorts of relationships, primarily because it applies a non-linear log transformation to the predicted odds ratio.
- The independent variables do *not* need to be multivariate normal (although multivariate normality is known to yield a more stable solution). Also the residuals (error) do not need to be multivariate normally distributed.
- **Homoscedasticity** is *not* required. That is, logistic regression does not need variances to be heteroscedastic for each level of the independent variables.

- Logistic regression can handle ordinal and nominal data as independent variables. That is, the independent variables do not need to be measured at the interval or ratio level.

Some assumptions, however, are retained. When logistic regression is used, keep the following requirements in mind:

- Logistic regression requires large sample sizes. Maximum Likelihood (ML) estimates are less powerful than OLS. Many researchers use a "rule of thumb" when using OLS: You need a bare minimum of 5 cases per independent variable in the analysis. A similar rule says that ML needs at least 10 cases per independent variable, with some researchers recommend at least 30 cases for each parameter to be estimated.
- Obviously, **binary logistic** regression requires the dependent variable to be binary and **ordinal logistic regression** requires the dependent variable to be ordinal. Reducing an ordinal or even a continuous variable to the dichotomous level throws away a lot of information. That makes binary logistic regression inferior compared to ordinal logistic regression in these cases.
- As with all statistical modeling, the model should be fitted correctly. Both "overfitting" and "underfitting" are problems. There are several statistical methods that aid in the selection of variables to include in a model. As with fitting OLS models, you should use theoretically driven modeling.
- Logistic regression requires each observation to be independent. That is that the data-points should not be from any *dependent* samples design (e.g., pretest-posttest designs, matching designs).
- The predictor variables should have little or no multicollinearity. That is, the independent variables should be independent from each other.

Logistic regression assumes linearity of independent variables and log odds. In other words, logistic regression does not require the dependent and independent variables to be related linearly (as does OLS), but it requires that the independent variables are linearly related to the *log odds*. Failure to meet this requirement can greatly diminish the power of hypothesis tests.

Adam J. McKee

Key Terms

Logistic regression, binary, odds ratio, ordinal logistic regression, Homoscedasticity

Section 7.4:
ANCOVA

When testing a hypothesis with ANOVA models, we end up with an F statistic, which is a "signal to noise ratio." Most of the noise is caused by individual differences among participants in the study. Logically, if we can differentiate between those random differences that cause variance and our experimental treatment that causes variance, we have a much more powerful statistical test. To continue our analogy, when we eliminate noise, the signal gets stronger.

Analysis of Covariance (ANCOVA) is an extension of ANOVA that provides a way of statistically controlling the (linear) effect of variables one does not want to examine in a study. In other words, the variable is thought to confound your results, and you want to rid your analysis of its effects. These extraneous variables are called **covariates**, or **control variables**. ANCOVA allows you to remove covariates from the list of possible explanations of the variance in the dependent variable. ANCOVA does this by using mathematical methods rather than experimental methods (e.g., good experimental design) to control extraneous variables.

ANCOVA is used in experimental studies when researchers want to remove the effects of some antecedent variable, such as preexisting conditions. For example, pretest scores are often used as covariates in pretest-posttest experimental designs (as is the analysis of *gain* or *difference scores*). ANCOVA is also used in non-experimental research, such as with surveys and nonrandom samples, or in quasi-experiments when subjects cannot be assigned randomly to control and experimental groups.

The basic ANCOVA model requires that these covariates be measured on at least the interval scale. If researchers are worried about a categorical variable, then a multi-way ANOVA can be used to treat the potential nuisance variable as a separate effect. The basic ANCOVA model requires that these covariates be measured on at least the interval scale. When the assumptions of ANCOVA can be met, the method improves the power of the subsequent test by removing systematic variance among subjects by subtracting it from the within-groups error term. Note that the increase in power only occurs if the covariate is actually correlated with the dependent variable. If the correlation is very weak or does not exist at all, then "throwing in" the covariate serves to reduce the power of the analysis. To calculate this, a regression coefficient is calculated to determine what variance is predictable in the DV by knowing the covariate; once that amount of variance is known, it can be subtracted. This significantly increases the signal to noise (F) ratio by reducing the noise in the denominator of the F ratio. The basic process starts just as a regular ANOVA would start, but an adjusted (for the covariate) sum of squares is computed for each component.

Key Terms

Analysis of Covariance (ANCOVA), covariate, statistical control, control variable

Section 7.5:
Structural Equation
Models (SEMs)

You can think of **Structural Equation Models** (SEMs) as an extension of the General Linear Model that proves to be more versatile and more powerful than multiple regression analysis. One way to think of SEMs is as a hybrid between *factor analysis* and *regression* analysis. Given the power and diversity of application, you shouldn't think of SEM in terms of a single statistical technique like a t-test or a correlation. It may be more helpful to think of it as a general modeling framework that can be customized to many different research questions. Rather than having a fixed structure, you can model many different structures depending on your research purpose.

SEMs have several known aliases:

-Causal modeling

-Latent variable models

-Models with unobserved variables

-Analysis of covariance structures

-Structural modeling

Because it is the most general method known to date, SEM is the most versatile analytical method available to researchers.

Figure 41. A Structural Equation Model.

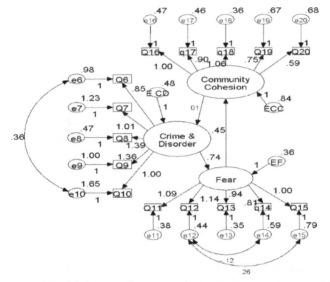

The above figure represents a structural equation model that depicts the relationships specified by the Broken Windows Theory. Note that the shapes represent different aspects of the model. The squares (rectangles) represent individual observed variables (survey responses). The ovals below each rectangle represent the **error terms**; in regression analysis, we pretend these don't exist most of the time. In SEM, they are explicitly modeled. The ovals represent the **latent constructs** that the **indicator variables** measure. The arrows from the ovals to the squares signify that the latent construct causes each of the survey responses. The number that goes with each arrow represents the linear relationship between the measured variable and the latent construct. The arrows between the ovals represent the relationships between the latent constructs. In the example, it is hypothesized that fear of crime causes a breakdown in community cohesion (informal social controls) and that in turn causes an increase in crime and disorder. Note that the arrows form a causal loop, which represents the "spiral of decay" that Broken Windows Theory suggests. This sort of loop cannot be modeled in path analysis, making SEM superior in that regard.

In SEM convention, straight arrows represent causal relationships that are directional. Curved arrows represent correlations where no causal direction is specified. When error terms are correlated, this can be accounted for in the model, whereas with regression analysis we assume they are not correlated. In the model above, then, we can see that Fear is hypothesized to cause Community Cohesion. We can also see that Community Cohesion is hypothesized to cause Crime and Disorder.

We can think of all of the squares connected to a single oval as a factor model, similar to what we would get if we did a factor analysis with all of the variables represented by the squares. In this study, we can see that that the model is composed of three factors, which are defined by the survey responses. We can think of the relationships specified between the latent variables (ovals) as separate regression models. This obviously allows us to model incredibly complex models with many different measurements related to the latent constructs.

Note that the graphical image presents the coefficients for each "path," but there are tons of other numbers that usually don't get printed in the journal article. SEMs produce a truly amazing amount of numbers and can be very difficult to interpret. Behind the scenes, the paths are specified by sets of equations. The hypothesized model under study can be tested statistically in a simultaneous analysis of the entire *system of variables* to determine the extent to which it is consistent with the data. The math was mind-blowing until the advent of the graphical interfaces we use today. The most popular of these is known as AMOS.

SEM a methodology that takes a confirmatory (hypothesis testing) approach to the analysis of a structural theory bearing on some phenomenon.

It can be viewed as a combination of factor analysis and regression analysis; if you don't have a good understanding of those methods, you will not get SEMs. The most important aspect of SEM is its ability to model the effects of latent variables (factors) on each other.

Note that all we said in previous sections about causation still applies. *Covariation is not causation.* *Theory* is paramount in the development of structural equation models, and SEM is best at disconfirming theories. It can only support causal theories, not prove them. A particular model may be consistent with the data and get causation wrong. Recall that a model is a mathematical representation of the theoretical conception under study. Models represent the relationships between the variables that are hypothesized in theory.

Structural equations summarize mathematically the impact of all relevant variables in the model on a single variable. Thus the equation for a particular variable is the sum of all variables that have arrows pointing to it.

Simple Models

Just because you can model the relationship between latent variables that are measured by multiple indicators doesn't mean that you must. You can also model relationships between **observed variables**, just like path analysis. Let us say that you are researching SAT scores, and want to examine the relationship between education, income, and SAT scores. Figure 42 below specifies such as relationship.

Figure 42. Structural Equation Model Predicting SAT Scores.

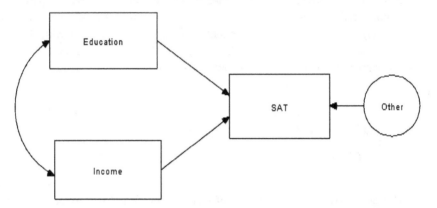

Note that the model indicates that education and income cause SAT scores; we know this because of the single-headed arrows pointing from the independent variables to the dependent variable. The curved arrow indicates that education and income will be correlated (because wealthier individuals tend to get more education). The "Other" represented by the circle is an error term; it is a circle because it was not observed, but rather it was estimated. This model would be more informative than an equivalent regression model because the error term is implicitly modeled rather than making the untenable assumption that it does not exist. Other than the minor "improvements" SEMs make, you can think of models like that as being identical to regression or path analysis.

"I strongly recommend that students try to set up any research problem under study in a path diagram. It forces one to conceptualize and bring out the basic structures of problems."

-Fred Kerlinger

The "one-way" arrows represent **Structural Regression Coefficients** and indicate the impact (effect) of one variable on another. As we discussed above, SEMs can model "causal loops." Models without such loops are said to be **recursive**.

Figure 43. A Simple Recursive Model.

Models that do specify causal loops are said to be Nonrecursive; Causal flow (arrows) go both ways, such as in causal loops or reciprocal causation.

Figure 44. A Simple Nonrecursive Model.

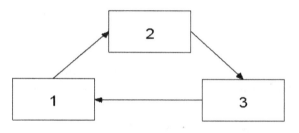

Variable Types

An **Exogenous variable**'s variation is assumed to be caused by influences *outside* the hypothesized model. No attempt is made to explain the variation of an exogenous variable or its relationship with other exogenous variables. In other words, no one headed arrows point to them. An endogenous variable, on the other hand, is a variable whose variation is explained in the model by exogenous or other endogenous variables. A one headed arrow points to them. This is very similar to the idea of independent and dependent variables, but is more versatile (generic).

Simple Regression

In SEM, endogenous variables are rarely ever perfectly related. Thus residuals (error, other) are included in the path diagram.

Figure 45. Simple Regression with SEMs.

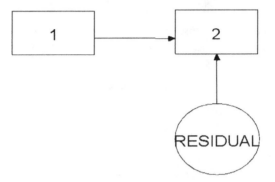

The above model indicates that 2 is caused by a linear combination of 1 and all other sources (residual). This is analogous to the regression equation:

$$Y' = \beta + Error$$

Identification

An important concept in SEMs is *identification*. **Identification** asks the question: Does the data provide enough information (sample moments-covariances) to find a unique solution for the structural parameters of the model? A **just identified model**, also known as an **exactly identified model**, is a model in which the number of equations is equal to the number of parameters to be estimated. Such models are perfectly reproduced by SEM (R2 = 1.0) and *have no value to the researcher*. Such models can never be rejected and have zero degrees of freedom. **Overidentified models** are models specified such that the model contains more information than is necessary to estimate path coefficients. Only overidentified models are appropriate to SEM. The model has one or more degrees of freedom.

Types of Effects

In ANOVA models, causes (IVs) are often called factors or effects. SEMs use the effects language, and the types of effects can be informative. A **direct effect** is a causal arrow *directly* from one variable to another. With An **indirect effect**, the effect of one variable on another is *through* a third variable. For example, in Figure 43 above, variable 1 has a *direct effect* on variable 2, but variable 1 has an *indirect effect* on variable 3 (because it flows through variable 2). The **total effect**, as you probably guessed, is equal to the direct plus the sum of indirect effects on a variable.

Model Testing

When testing a causal model, the researcher's objective is ascertaining whether the hypothesized model is consistent with the pattern of relationships among the variables under consideration. Mathematically, this can be determined by estimating the "**goodness of fit**." In this process, estimated parameters and constraints are used to calculate a *predicted* matrix of association. This is analogous to regression where we subtract a predicted value from an observed value to obtain a residual. The principle is simple: The smaller the residuals, the better the fit; the larger the residuals, the poorer the fit. We can perform a statistical significance test of the fit using the chi-square distribution.

In SEM, Chi-square is really a "badness of fit" measure. That is, the null hypothesis is that the model does not differ significantly from the data. In short, *we do not want to reject the null hypothesis*. Chi-square is almost always reported in SEM studies but is rarely considered alone as a measure of fit. Chi-square is strongly influenced by sample size. Adequate sample sizes for SEM analyses will be significant most of the time. Chi-square is very sensitive to departures from multivariate normality. This is why researchers using SEMs have derived several **fit indices** that are designed to correct the shortcomings of the chi-square statistic.

The **Goodness of Fit Index (GFI)** is roughly analogous to R^2 in multiple regression analysis. The **Adjusted Goodness of Fit (AGFI)** is calculated and interpreted similarly to the GFI, but provides a penalty for model complexity. This is to preserve the importance of **parsimony**. Both indices have ranges from zero to one; closer to one meaning better fit. A common rule of thumb is that values of .92 to .95 suggests good fit. These are sensitive to sample size and should be interpreted with caution.

The **Parsimony Goodness of Fit Index (PGFI)** seeks to balance parsimony and goodness of fit in one index. This was the first of many parsimony-based fit indices to be developed. As a rule of thumb, a PGFI > .5 suggests good fit.

Often, the researcher can compare two different models and determine which fits better, such as when there are two related but different theories to explain a phenomenon. There are actually several **comparative fit indices** in this family. This family of indices compares the hypothetical model to a baseline model rather than the absence of a model as does the GFI and AGFI. The **Normed Fit Index (NFI)** – Underestimates fit for small samples. The **Comparative Fit Index (CFI)** is a modification of the NFI designed to correct underestimation errors. Both the NFI and CFI range from zero to one. A rule of thumb for is that values of NIF/CFI > .95 suggest a good fit.

In AMOS, fit statistics are presented in three rows:

-First Row: The Hypothesized Model

-Second Row: Saturated Model

-Third Row: Independent Model

The **independent model** is a model where all correlations among variables are zero (they are independent in the sense of being orthogonal). This is the most restricted model. In a **saturated model**, the number of estimated parameters is equal to the data points. That is, the model is just identified. This is the least restricted model.

Plausible alternative models (based on alternative theoretical considerations) should be tested whenever possible. Do not interpret findings that a model fits the data as meaning that it is the only model that can do so. Alternative models represent competing hypotheses that must be ruled out. Researchers sometimes respecify their models, for two primary reasons to respecify a model: to increase parsimony and to improve model fit. Note that model revision is a *post hoc* process, and is thus *exploratory*. The results of such modified models are weak support for theory. The theoretical implications of such analyses should be tested using confirmatory techniques on *new* data.

Latent Variables

Recall that *latent variables* are constructs that cannot be directly measured by the researcher. Public Attitudes toward the police, anxiety, and intelligence are examples. Usually, the researcher will measure multiple indicators as a measure of such constructs. Think about how an IQ test works—lots of questions are used to get at one idea that is summarized as an "IQ Score." In multiple regression and path analysis, multiple indicators are treated as distinct variables. This causes problems with collinearity. SEMs are superior in this regard. SEM works best with multiple indicators—this is an important part of the measurement submodel. Three or more "good" indicators are preferable.

Path Coefficients

Path coefficients are number that are analogous to b and beta weights in regression analysis; they usually appear over the arrows in the path diagram. **Standardized structural coefficients** are what researchers are usually referring to when path coefficients are spoken of without qualification, most often it is the standardized form. As with OLS, these are important in comparing relative strengths of relationships. These are measured in standard deviation units. Unstandardized coefficients are based on covariances and have no common metric.

Correlated Error Terms

Error terms are correlated when the indicators measure something else or something in addition to the constructs they are supposed to measure. Every correlated error term must be interpreted substantively.

Models

The **measurement model** is the part of an SEM that contains latent variables and their indicators. Educationists and psychologists familiar with tests and measurement will understand this intuitively. The measurement model is also known as the Confirmatory Factor Analysis Model and Null Model. Paths from latent variables to the indicators are modeled, as are the paths form the error terms to the measured variables. In these types of models, there are no paths (direct effects) between the latent variables specified.

The structural model is model Components connecting unobserved (latent) components with each other. **Model specification errors** refer to using the wrong or an inappropriate model. This can happen in several ways: Omitting relevant variables, including irrelevant variables, postulating linear model when nonlinear more appropriate, and introducing measurement error are among the most common.

Key Terms

Structural Equation Models, error terms, latent constructs, indicator variables, observed variables, structural regression coefficients, recursive, non-recursive, exogenous variable, direct effect, indirect effect, total effect, goodness of fit, fit indices, Goodness of Fix Index (GFI), Adjusted Goodness of Fit (AGFI), parsimony, Parsimony Goodness of Fit Index (PGFI), comparative fit indices, Normed Fit Index (NFI), Comparative Fit Index (CFI), independent model, saturated model, path coefficients, standardized structural coefficients, measurement model, model specification errors

Appendix A:
Significance of Pearson's *r*

df	.05 Level	.01 Level
1	.996	.999
2	.950	.990
3	.878	.956
4	.811	.917
5	.754	.874
6	.707	.834
7	.666	.798
8	.632	.765
9	.602	.735
10	.576	.708
11	.553	.684
12	.532	.661
13	.514	.641
14	.497	.623
15	.482	.606
16	.468	.590
17	.456	.575
18	.444	.561
19	.433	.549
20	.423	.537
25	.381	.487
30	.349	.449
35	.325	.418
40	.304	.393
45	.288	.372
50	.273	.354
60	.250	.325
70	.232	.302

Adam J. McKee

Appendix B:
Critical Values
of Chi Square

df	0.05 Level	0.01 Level	0.001 Level
1	3.841	6.635	10.828
2	5.991	9.210	13.816
3	7.815	11.345	16.266
4	9.488	13.277	18.467
5	11.070	15.086	20.515
6	12.592	16.812	22.458
7	14.067	18.475	24.322
8	15.507	20.090	26.125
9	16.919	21.666	27.877
10	18.307	23.209	29.588
11	19.675	24.725	31.264
12	21.026	26.217	32.910
13	22.362	27.688	34.528
14	23.685	29.141	36.123
15	24.996	30.578	37.697
16	26.296	32.000	39.252
17	27.587	33.409	40.790
18	28.869	34.805	42.312
19	30.144	36.191	43.820
20	31.410	37.566	45.315
21	32.671	38.932	46.797
22	33.924	40.289	48.268
23	35.172	41.638	49.728
24	36.415	42.980	51.179
25	37.652	44.314	52.620
26	38.885	45.642	54.052
27	40.113	46.963	55.476
28	41.337	48.278	56.892

Appendix C: Critical Values for Student's t

df	0.10	0.05	0.025	0.01	0.005	0.001
1.	3.078	6.314	12.706	31.821	63.657	318.313
2.	1.886	2.920	4.303	6.965	9.925	22.327
3.	1.638	2.353	3.182	4.541	5.841	10.215
4.	1.533	2.132	2.776	3.747	4.604	7.173
5.	1.476	2.015	2.571	3.365	4.032	5.893
6.	1.440	1.943	2.447	3.143	3.707	5.208
7.	1.415	1.895	2.365	2.998	3.499	4.782
8.	1.397	1.860	2.306	2.896	3.355	4.499
9.	1.383	1.833	2.262	2.821	3.250	4.296
10.	1.372	1.812	2.228	2.764	3.169	4.143
11.	1.363	1.796	2.201	2.718	3.106	4.024
12.	1.356	1.782	2.179	2.681	3.055	3.929
13.	1.350	1.771	2.160	2.650	3.012	3.852
14.	1.345	1.761	2.145	2.624	2.977	3.787
15.	1.341	1.753	2.131	2.602	2.947	3.733
16.	1.337	1.746	2.120	2.583	2.921	3.686
17.	1.333	1.740	2.110	2.567	2.898	3.646
18.	1.330	1.734	2.101	2.552	2.878	3.610
19.	1.328	1.729	2.093	2.539	2.861	3.579
20.	1.325	1.725	2.086	2.528	2.845	3.552
21.	1.323	1.721	2.080	2.518	2.831	3.527
22.	1.321	1.717	2.074	2.508	2.819	3.505
23.	1.319	1.714	2.069	2.500	2.807	3.485
24.	1.318	1.711	2.064	2.492	2.797	3.467
25.	1.316	1.708	2.060	2.485	2.787	3.450
26.	1.315	1.706	2.056	2.479	2.779	3.435
27.	1.314	1.703	2.052	2.473	2.771	3.421
28.	1.313	1.701	2.048	2.467	2.763	3.408
29.	1.311	1.699	2.045	2.462	2.756	3.396

Critical Values for Student's t Distribution (Cont.)

df	0.10	0.05	0.025	0.01	0.005	0.001
30.	1.310	1.697	2.042	2.457	2.750	3.385
31.	1.309	1.696	2.040	2.453	2.744	3.375
32.	1.309	1.694	2.037	2.449	2.738	3.365
33.	1.308	1.692	2.035	2.445	2.733	3.356
34.	1.307	1.691	2.032	2.441	2.728	3.348
35.	1.306	1.690	2.030	2.438	2.724	3.340
36.	1.306	1.688	2.028	2.434	2.719	3.333
37.	1.305	1.687	2.026	2.431	2.715	3.326
38.	1.304	1.686	2.024	2.429	2.712	3.319
39.	1.304	1.685	2.023	2.426	2.708	3.313
40.	1.303	1.684	2.021	2.423	2.704	3.307
41.	1.303	1.683	2.020	2.421	2.701	3.301
42.	1.302	1.682	2.018	2.418	2.698	3.296
43.	1.302	1.681	2.017	2.416	2.695	3.291
44.	1.301	1.680	2.015	2.414	2.692	3.286
45.	1.301	1.679	2.014	2.412	2.690	3.281
46.	1.300	1.679	2.013	2.410	2.687	3.277
47.	1.300	1.678	2.012	2.408	2.685	3.273
48.	1.299	1.677	2.011	2.407	2.682	3.269
49.	1.299	1.677	2.010	2.405	2.680	3.265
50.	1.299	1.676	2.009	2.403	2.678	3.261
51.	1.298	1.675	2.008	2.402	2.676	3.258
52.	1.298	1.675	2.007	2.400	2.674	3.255
53.	1.298	1.674	2.006	2.399	2.672	3.251
54.	1.297	1.674	2.005	2.397	2.670	3.248
55.	1.297	1.673	2.004	2.396	2.668	3.245
56.	1.297	1.673	2.003	2.395	2.667	3.242
57.	1.297	1.672	2.002	2.394	2.665	3.239
58.	1.296	1.672	2.002	2.392	2.663	3.237
59.	1.296	1.671	2.001	2.391	2.662	3.234
60.	1.296	1.671	2.000	2.390	2.660	3.232

Critical Values for Student's t Distribution (Cont.)

df	0.10	0.05	0.025	0.01	0.005	0.001
61.	1.296	1.670	2.000	2.389	2.659	3.229
62.	1.295	1.670	1.999	2.388	2.657	3.227
63.	1.295	1.669	1.998	2.387	2.656	3.225
64.	1.295	1.669	1.998	2.386	2.655	3.223
65.	1.295	1.669	1.997	2.385	2.654	3.220
66.	1.295	1.668	1.997	2.384	2.652	3.218
67.	1.294	1.668	1.996	2.383	2.651	3.216
68.	1.294	1.668	1.995	2.382	2.650	3.214
69.	1.294	1.667	1.995	2.382	2.649	3.213
70.	1.294	1.667	1.994	2.381	2.648	3.211
71.	1.294	1.667	1.994	2.380	2.647	3.209
72.	1.293	1.666	1.993	2.379	2.646	3.207
73.	1.293	1.666	1.993	2.379	2.645	3.206
74.	1.293	1.666	1.993	2.378	2.644	3.204
75.	1.293	1.665	1.992	2.377	2.643	3.202
76.	1.293	1.665	1.992	2.376	2.642	3.201
77.	1.293	1.665	1.991	2.376	2.641	3.199
78.	1.292	1.665	1.991	2.375	2.640	3.198
79.	1.292	1.664	1.990	2.374	2.640	3.197
80.	1.292	1.664	1.990	2.374	2.639	3.195
81.	1.292	1.664	1.990	2.373	2.638	3.194
82.	1.292	1.664	1.989	2.373	2.637	3.193
83.	1.292	1.663	1.989	2.372	2.636	3.191
84.	1.292	1.663	1.989	2.372	2.636	3.190
85.	1.292	1.663	1.988	2.371	2.635	3.189
86.	1.291	1.663	1.988	2.370	2.634	3.188
87.	1.291	1.663	1.988	2.370	2.634	3.187
88.	1.291	1.662	1.987	2.369	2.633	3.185
89.	1.291	1.662	1.987	2.369	2.632	3.184
90.	1.291	1.662	1.987	2.368	2.632	3.183

Critical Values for Student's *t* Distribution (Cont.)

df	0.10	0.05	0.025	0.01	0.005	0.001
91.	1.291	1.662	1.986	2.368	2.631	3.182
92.	1.291	1.662	1.986	2.368	2.630	3.181
93.	1.291	1.661	1.986	2.367	2.630	3.180
94.	1.291	1.661	1.986	2.367	2.629	3.179
95.	1.291	1.661	1.985	2.366	2.629	3.178
96.	1.290	1.661	1.985	2.366	2.628	3.177
97.	1.290	1.661	1.985	2.365	2.627	3.176
98.	1.290	1.661	1.984	2.365	2.627	3.175
99.	1.290	1.660	1.984	2.365	2.626	3.175
100.	1.290	1.660	1.984	2.364	2.626	3.174
Infinity	1.282	1.645	1.960	2.326	2.576	3.090

Appendix D: Critical Values of F (.05 Level)

Note: The numerator degrees of freedom (between groups) run across the top of the table, and the denominator degrees of freedom (within groups) run up and down.

df	1	2	3	4	5	6	7	8	9	10
1	161.448	199.500	215.707	224.583	230.162	233.986	236.768	238.882	240.543	241.882
2	18.513	19.000	19.164	19.247	19.296	19.330	19.353	19.371	19.385	19.396
3	10.128	9.552	9.277	9.117	9.013	8.941	8.887	8.845	8.812	8.786
4	7.709	6.944	6.591	6.388	6.256	6.163	6.094	6.041	5.999	5.964
5	6.608	5.786	5.409	5.192	5.050	4.950	4.876	4.818	4.772	4.735
6	5.987	5.143	4.757	4.534	4.387	4.284	4.207	4.147	4.099	4.060
7	5.591	4.737	4.347	4.120	3.972	3.866	3.787	3.726	3.677	3.637
8	5.318	4.459	4.066	3.838	3.687	3.581	3.500	3.438	3.388	3.347
9	5.117	4.256	3.863	3.633	3.482	3.374	3.293	3.230	3.179	3.137
10	4.965	4.103	3.708	3.478	3.326	3.217	3.135	3.072	3.020	2.978
11	4.844	3.982	3.587	3.357	3.204	3.095	3.012	2.948	2.896	2.854
12	4.747	3.885	3.490	3.259	3.106	2.996	2.913	2.849	2.796	2.753
13	4.667	3.806	3.411	3.179	3.025	2.915	2.832	2.767	2.714	2.671
14	4.600	3.739	3.344	3.112	2.958	2.848	2.764	2.699	2.646	2.602
15	4.543	3.682	3.287	3.056	2.901	2.790	2.707	2.641	2.588	2.544
16	4.494	3.634	3.239	3.007	2.852	2.741	2.657	2.591	2.538	2.494
17	4.451	3.592	3.197	2.965	2.810	2.699	2.614	2.548	2.494	2.450
18	4.414	3.555	3.160	2.928	2.773	2.661	2.577	2.510	2.456	2.412
19	4.381	3.522	3.127	2.895	2.740	2.628	2.544	2.477	2.423	2.378
20	4.351	3.493	3.098	2.866	2.711	2.599	2.514	2.447	2.393	2.348
21	4.325	3.467	3.072	2.840	2.685	2.573	2.488	2.420	2.366	2.321
22	4.301	3.443	3.049	2.817	2.661	2.549	2.464	2.397	2.342	2.297
23	4.279	3.422	3.028	2.796	2.640	2.528	2.442	2.375	2.320	2.275
24	4.260	3.403	3.009	2.776	2.621	2.508	2.423	2.355	2.300	2.255
25	4.242	3.385	2.991	2.759	2.603	2.490	2.405	2.337	2.282	2.236

Critical Values of *F* at the .05 Level (Cont.)

df	1	2	3	4	5	6	7	8	9	10
26	4.225	3.369	2.975	2.743	2.587	2.474	2.388	2.321	2.265	2.220
27	4.210	3.354	2.960	2.728	2.572	2.459	2.373	2.305	2.250	2.204
28	4.196	3.340	2.947	2.714	2.558	2.445	2.359	2.291	2.236	2.190
29	4.183	3.328	2.934	2.701	2.545	2.432	2.346	2.278	2.223	2.177
30	4.171	3.316	2.922	2.690	2.534	2.421	2.334	2.266	2.211	2.165
31	4.160	3.305	2.911	2.679	2.523	2.409	2.323	2.255	2.199	2.153
32	4.149	3.295	2.901	2.668	2.512	2.399	2.313	2.244	2.189	2.142
33	4.139	3.285	2.892	2.659	2.503	2.389	2.303	2.235	2.179	2.133
34	4.130	3.276	2.883	2.650	2.494	2.380	2.294	2.225	2.170	2.123
35	4.121	3.267	2.874	2.641	2.485	2.372	2.285	2.217	2.161	2.114
36	4.113	3.259	2.866	2.634	2.477	2.364	2.277	2.209	2.153	2.106
37	4.105	3.252	2.859	2.626	2.470	2.356	2.270	2.201	2.145	2.098
38	4.098	3.245	2.852	2.619	2.463	2.349	2.262	2.194	2.138	2.091
39	4.091	3.238	2.845	2.612	2.456	2.342	2.255	2.187	2.131	2.084
40	4.085	3.232	2.839	2.606	2.449	2.336	2.249	2.180	2.124	2.077
41	4.079	3.226	2.833	2.600	2.443	2.330	2.243	2.174	2.118	2.071
42	4.073	3.220	2.827	2.594	2.438	2.324	2.237	2.168	2.112	2.065
43	4.067	3.214	2.822	2.589	2.432	2.318	2.232	2.163	2.106	2.059
44	4.062	3.209	2.816	2.584	2.427	2.313	2.226	2.157	2.101	2.054
45	4.057	3.204	2.812	2.579	2.422	2.308	2.221	2.152	2.096	2.049
46	4.052	3.200	2.807	2.574	2.417	2.304	2.216	2.147	2.091	2.044
47	4.047	3.195	2.802	2.570	2.413	2.299	2.212	2.143	2.086	2.039
48	4.043	3.191	2.798	2.565	2.409	2.295	2.207	2.138	2.082	2.035
49	4.038	3.187	2.794	2.561	2.404	2.290	2.203	2.134	2.077	2.030
50	4.034	3.183	2.790	2.557	2.400	2.286	2.199	2.130	2.073	2.026

Critical Values of *F* at the .05 Level (Cont.)

df	1	2	3	4	5	6	7	8	9	10
51	4.030	3.179	2.786	2.553	2.397	2.283	2.195	2.126	2.069	2.022
52	4.027	3.175	2.783	2.550	2.393	2.279	2.192	2.122	2.066	2.018
53	4.023	3.172	2.779	2.546	2.389	2.275	2.188	2.119	2.062	2.015
54	4.020	3.168	2.776	2.543	2.386	2.272	2.185	2.115	2.059	2.011
55	4.016	3.165	2.773	2.540	2.383	2.269	2.181	2.112	2.055	2.008
56	4.013	3.162	2.769	2.537	2.380	2.266	2.178	2.109	2.052	2.005
57	4.010	3.159	2.766	2.534	2.377	2.263	2.175	2.106	2.049	2.001
58	4.007	3.156	2.764	2.531	2.374	2.260	2.172	2.103	2.046	1.998
59	4.004	3.153	2.761	2.528	2.371	2.257	2.169	2.100	2.043	1.995
60	4.001	3.150	2.758	2.525	2.368	2.254	2.167	2.097	2.040	1.993
61	3.998	3.148	2.755	2.523	2.366	2.251	2.164	2.094	2.037	1.990
62	3.996	3.145	2.753	2.520	2.363	2.249	2.161	2.092	2.035	1.987
63	3.993	3.143	2.751	2.518	2.361	2.246	2.159	2.089	2.032	1.985
64	3.991	3.140	2.748	2.515	2.358	2.244	2.156	2.087	2.030	1.982
65	3.989	3.138	2.746	2.513	2.356	2.242	2.154	2.084	2.027	1.980
66	3.986	3.136	2.744	2.511	2.354	2.239	2.152	2.082	2.025	1.977
67	3.984	3.134	2.742	2.509	2.352	2.237	2.150	2.080	2.023	1.975
68	3.982	3.132	2.740	2.507	2.350	2.235	2.148	2.078	2.021	1.973
69	3.980	3.130	2.737	2.505	2.348	2.233	2.145	2.076	2.019	1.971
70	3.978	3.128	2.736	2.503	2.346	2.231	2.143	2.074	2.017	1.969
71	3.976	3.126	2.734	2.501	2.344	2.229	2.142	2.072	2.015	1.967
72	3.974	3.124	2.732	2.499	2.342	2.227	2.140	2.070	2.013	1.965
73	3.972	3.122	2.730	2.497	2.340	2.226	2.138	2.068	2.011	1.963
74	3.970	3.120	2.728	2.495	2.338	2.224	2.136	2.066	2.009	1.961
75	3.968	3.119	2.727	2.494	2.337	2.222	2.134	2.064	2.007	1.959

Adam J. McKee

Critical Values of *F* at the .05 Level (Cont.)

df	1	2	3	4	5	6	7	8	9	10
76	3.967	3.117	2.725	2.492	2.335	2.220	2.133	2.063	2.006	1.958
77	3.965	3.115	2.723	2.490	2.333	2.219	2.131	2.061	2.004	1.956
78	3.963	3.114	2.722	2.489	2.332	2.217	2.129	2.059	2.002	1.954
79	3.962	3.112	2.720	2.487	2.330	2.216	2.128	2.058	2.001	1.953
80	3.960	3.111	2.719	2.486	2.329	2.214	2.126	2.056	1.999	1.951
81	3.959	3.109	2.717	2.484	2.327	2.213	2.125	2.055	1.998	1.950
82	3.957	3.108	2.716	2.483	2.326	2.211	2.123	2.053	1.996	1.948
83	3.956	3.107	2.715	2.482	2.324	2.210	2.122	2.052	1.995	1.947
84	3.955	3.105	2.713	2.480	2.323	2.209	2.121	2.051	1.993	1.945
85	3.953	3.104	2.712	2.479	2.322	2.207	2.119	2.049	1.992	1.944
86	3.952	3.103	2.711	2.478	2.321	2.206	2.118	2.048	1.991	1.943
87	3.951	3.101	2.709	2.476	2.319	2.205	2.117	2.047	1.989	1.941
88	3.949	3.100	2.708	2.475	2.318	2.203	2.115	2.045	1.988	1.940
89	3.948	3.099	2.707	2.474	2.317	2.202	2.114	2.044	1.987	1.939
90	3.947	3.098	2.706	2.473	2.316	2.201	2.113	2.043	1.986	1.938
91	3.946	3.097	2.705	2.472	2.315	2.200	2.112	2.042	1.984	1.936
92	3.945	3.095	2.704	2.471	2.313	2.199	2.111	2.041	1.983	1.935
93	3.943	3.094	2.703	2.470	2.312	2.198	2.110	2.040	1.982	1.934
94	3.942	3.093	2.701	2.469	2.311	2.197	2.109	2.038	1.981	1.933
95	3.941	3.092	2.700	2.467	2.310	2.196	2.108	2.037	1.980	1.932
96	3.940	3.091	2.699	2.466	2.309	2.195	2.106	2.036	1.979	1.931
97	3.939	3.090	2.698	2.465	2.308	2.194	2.105	2.035	1.978	1.930
98	3.938	3.089	2.697	2.465	2.307	2.193	2.104	2.034	1.977	1.929
99	3.937	3.088	2.696	2.464	2.306	2.192	2.103	2.033	1.976	1.928
100	3.936	3.087	2.696	2.463	2.305	2.191	2.103	2.032	1.975	1.927

Appendix E: Studentized Range Statistic (q)

df	2	3	4	5	6	7	8	9	10	11	12
5	3.64	4.60	5.22	5.67	6.03	6.33	6.58	6.80	6.99	7.17	7.32
6	3.46	4.34	4.90	5.30	5.63	5.90	6.12	6.32	6.49	6.65	6.79
7	3.34	4.16	4.68	5.06	5.36	5.61	5.82	6.00	6.16	6.30	6.43
8	3.26	4.04	4.53	4.89	5.17	5.40	5.60	5.77	5.92	6.05	6.18
9	3.20	3.95	4.41	4.76	5.02	5.24	5.43	5.59	5.74	5.87	5.98
10	3.15	3.88	4.33	4.65	4.91	5.12	5.30	5.46	5.60	5.72	5.83
11	3.11	3.82	4.26	4.57	4.82	5.03	5.20	5.35	5.49	5.61	5.71
12	3.08	3.77	4.20	4.51	4.75	4.95	5.12	5.27	5.39	5.51	5.61
13	3.06	3.73	4.15	4.45	4.69	4.88	5.05	5.19	5.32	5.43	5.53
14	3.03	3.70	4.11	4.41	4.64	4.83	4.99	5.13	5.25	5.36	5.46
15	3.01	3.67	4.08	4.37	4.59	4.78	4.94	5.08	5.20	5.31	5.40
16	3.00	3.65	4.05	4.33	4.56	4.74	4.90	5.03	5.15	5.26	5.35
17	2.98	3.63	4.02	4.30	4.52	4.70	4.86	4.99	5.11	5.21	5.31
18	2.97	3.61	4.00	4.28	4.49	4.67	4.82	4.96	5.07	5.17	5.27
19	2.96	3.59	3.98	4.25	4.47	4.65	4.79	4.92	5.04	5.14	5.23
20	2.95	3.58	3.96	4.23	4.45	4.62	4.77	4.90	5.01	5.11	5.20
30	2.89	3.49	3.85	4.10	4.30	4.46	4.60	4.72	4.82	4.92	5.00
40	2.86	3.44	3.79	4.04	4.23	4.39	4.52	4.63	4.73	7.82	4.90
60	2.83	3.40	3.74	3.98	4.16	4.31	4.44	4.55	4.65	4.73	4.81
120	2.80	3.36	3.68	3.92	4.10	4.24	4.36	4.47	4.56	4.64	4.71
Infinity	2.77	3.31	3.63	3.86	4.03	4.17	4.29	4.39	4.47	4.55	4.62

Adam J. McKee

Appendix F: Standard Normal Distribution Table

Note. This table is used to fine the area under the curve between the mean and any z-score up to 3.00. Find the whole number and the tenths place for the z-score that you are trying to find by going down the table. Find the one-hundredths place you are looking for by going across the table. For example, if I want to find the area under the curve between the mean and a z-score of 1.96, I trace down the column until I get to the 1.9 row, then across until I get to 0.06 and find the value of 0.4750. To find the area on either side of the mean for that z-score, multiply the value by two. In our example, we multiply .4750 by 2 to get 0.9500. Thus, 95% of cases fall within 1.96 standard deviations from the mean.

z	0.00	0.01	0.02	0.03	0.04	0.05	0.06	0.07	0.08	0.09
0.0	0.0000	0.0040	0.0080	0.0120	0.0160	0.0199	0.0239	0.0279	0.0319	0.0359
0.1	0.0398	0.0438	0.0478	0.0517	0.0557	0.0596	0.0636	0.0675	0.0714	0.0753
0.2	0.0793	0.0832	0.0871	0.0910	0.0948	0.0987	0.1026	0.1064	0.1103	0.1141
0.3	0.1179	0.1217	0.1255	0.1293	0.1331	0.1368	0.1406	0.1443	0.1480	0.1517
0.4	0.1554	0.1591	0.1628	0.1664	0.1700	0.1736	0.1772	0.1808	0.1844	0.1879
0.5	0.1915	0.1950	0.1985	0.2019	0.2054	0.2088	0.2123	0.2157	0.2190	0.2224
0.6	0.2257	0.2291	0.2324	0.2357	0.2389	0.2422	0.2454	0.2486	0.2517	0.2549
0.7	0.2580	0.2611	0.2642	0.2673	0.2704	0.2734	0.2764	0.2794	0.2823	0.2852
0.8	0.2881	0.2910	0.2939	0.2967	0.2995	0.3023	0.3051	0.3078	0.3106	0.3133
0.9	0.3159	0.3186	0.3212	0.3238	0.3264	0.3289	0.3315	0.3340	0.3365	0.3389
1.0	0.3413	0.3438	0.3461	0.3485	0.3508	0.3531	0.3554	0.3577	0.3599	0.3621
1.1	0.3643	0.3665	0.3686	0.3708	0.3729	0.3749	0.3770	0.3790	0.3810	0.3830
1.2	0.3849	0.3869	0.3888	0.3907	0.3925	0.3944	0.3962	0.3980	0.3997	0.4015
1.3	0.4032	0.4049	0.4066	0.4082	0.4099	0.4115	0.4131	0.4147	0.4162	0.4177
1.4	0.4192	0.4207	0.4222	0.4236	0.4251	0.4265	0.4279	0.4292	0.4306	0.4319
1.5	0.4332	0.4345	0.4357	0.4370	0.4382	0.4394	0.4406	0.4418	0.4429	0.4441

Standard Normal Distribution Table (Cont.)

z	0.00	0.01	0.02	0.03	0.04	0.05	0.06	0.07	0.08	0.09
1.6	0.4452	0.4463	0.4474	0.4484	0.4495	0.4505	0.4515	0.4525	0.4535	0.4545
1.7	0.4554	0.4564	0.4573	0.4582	0.4591	0.4599	0.4608	0.4616	0.4625	0.4633
1.8	0.4641	0.4649	0.4656	0.4664	0.4671	0.4678	0.4686	0.4693	0.4699	0.4706
1.9	0.4713	0.4719	0.4726	0.4732	0.4738	0.4744	0.4750	0.4756	0.4761	0.4767
2.0	0.4772	0.4778	0.4783	0.4788	0.4793	0.4798	0.4803	0.4808	0.4812	0.4817
2.1	0.4821	0.4826	0.4830	0.4834	0.4838	0.4842	0.4846	0.4850	0.4854	0.4857
2.2	0.4861	0.4864	0.4868	0.4871	0.4875	0.4878	0.4881	0.4884	0.4887	0.4890
2.3	0.4893	0.4896	0.4898	0.4901	0.4904	0.4906	0.4909	0.4911	0.4913	0.4916
2.4	0.4918	0.4920	0.4922	0.4925	0.4927	0.4929	0.4931	0.4932	0.4934	0.4936
2.5	0.4938	0.4940	0.4941	0.4943	0.4945	0.4946	0.4948	0.4949	0.4951	0.4952
2.6	0.4953	0.4955	0.4956	0.4957	0.4959	0.4960	0.4961	0.4962	0.4963	0.4964
2.7	0.4965	0.4966	0.4967	0.4968	0.4969	0.4970	0.4971	0.4972	0.4973	0.4974
2.8	0.4974	0.4975	0.4976	0.4977	0.4977	0.4978	0.4979	0.4979	0.4980	0.4981
2.9	0.4981	0.4982	0.4982	0.4983	0.4984	0.4984	0.4985	0.4985	0.4986	0.4986
3.0	0.4987	0.4987	0.4987	0.4988	0.4988	0.4989	0.4989	0.4989	0.4990	0.4990

Note that the shaded cells represent the values for the 68% Rule, the 95% Rule, and the 99% Rule.

References

Allison, P. D. (1999). *Multiple regression: A primer.* Thousand Oaks, CA: Sage.

Cook, T. D. & Campbell, D. T. (1979). Quasi-*experimentation: Design and analysis issues for field settings.* Boston: Houghton Mifflin.

Fox, J. (1997). Applied *regression analysis, linear models, and related methods.* Thousand Oaks, CA: Sage.

Pearl, J. (2009). Causal inference in statistics: An overview. *Statistics Surveys, 3,* 96 – 146. DOI: 10.1214/09-SS057

Pedhazur, E. J. (1997). *Multiple regression in behavioral research: Explanation and prediction* (3rd Ed.). New York: Harcourt Brace.